By George Santayana

PERSONS AND PLACES: THE BACKGROUND OF MY LIFE

THE MIDDLE SPAN: VOL. II OF PERSONS AND PLACES

REALMS OF BEING

THE REALM OF SPIRIT

THE REALM OF TRUTH

THE PHILOSOPHY OF SANTAYANA: SELECTIONS FROM THE WORKS
OF GEORGE SANTAYANA

OBITER SCRIPTA: LECTURES, ESSAYS AND REVIEWS

THE LAST PURITAN: A MEMOIR IN THE FORM OF A NOVEL

SOME TURNS OF THOUGHT IN MODERN PHILOSOPHY

THE GENTEEL TRADITION AT BAY

THE REALM OF ESSENCE

THE REALM OF MATTER

PLATONISM AND THE SPIRITUAL LIFE

DIALOGUES IN LIMBO

POEMS

SCEPTICISM AND ANIMAL FAITH

EGOTISM IN GERMAN PHILOSOPHY

SOLILOQUIES IN ENGLAND AND LATER SOLILOQUIES

CHARACTER AND OPINION IN THE UNITED STATES

THE SENSE OF BEAUTY

INTERPRETATIONS OF POETRY AND RELIGION

THE HERMIT OF CARMEL AND OTHER POEMS

WINDS OF DOCTRINE

THE LIFE OF REASON: OR THE PHASES OF HUMAN PROGRESS

    I.   Introduction and Reason in Common Sense
   II.   Reason in Society
  III.   Reason in Religion
  IV.   Reason in Art
   V.   Reason in Science

LITTLE ESSAYS DRAWN FROM THE WORKS OF GEORGE SANTAYANA
By Logan Pearsall Smith, *with the collaboration of the author*.

Charles Scribner's Sons

THE MIDDLE SPAN

GEORGE SANTAYANA

The MIDDLE SPAN

VOL. II

Persons and Places

BY
GEORGE SANTAYANA

NEW YORK
CHARLES SCRIBNER'S SONS
1945

CONTENTS

THE MIDDLE SPAN

CHAPTER I

GERMANY

THE impulse that sent me to study in Germany came from America—something for which America is to be thanked; yet the failure of that adventure in my case was connected with its origin. I was too much enveloped in my American (and afterwards in my English) associations to lose myself in the German scene, to learn German properly, and to turn a copious German "spiritual" stream into my private channel. In my Germany there was, and there still is, too much of me and too little of Germany.

Some recommendation that I have forgotten led me in the early autumn of 1886 to Göttingen, with the idea of learning a little more German than the very little that I knew. I lived in a boarding-house kept by Frau Pastorin Schlote, whose elderly daughter —not the Irma of *The Last Puritan*, who is imaginary—knew English and gave the foreign boarders lessons in German. I learned enough to understand lectures and formal conversation from the first; but there was no one with whom I could begin to talk, and with my dislike of drudgery, I turned rather to deciphering for myself, with the help of a grammar and a dictionary, texts that were worth reading on their own account: *Deutsche Lyrik*, Heine and *Wilhelm Meister*. I made good progress of a sort, for my own ends, but without thoroughness; and my tongue remained torpid and my inflections inaccurate. *"Sie sprechen sehr nett,"* the superior housekeeper said one day when I excused myself, *"die Endungen aber fehlen."* Two or three months later in Berlin my landlady and her friends one day were discussing me, when her daughter observed that I was in my room and could hear them

I

through the thin door. *"Der versteht ja nichts,"* her mother cried impatiently, and went on wondering at my solitary life, that I went out for a walk alone and all the rest of the day sat working in my room. I understood every word perfectly: but in conversation I was helpless; there were no people with whom I cared to talk; and my punishment was that I never learned to speak the language.

From Göttingen I went to Dresden where Herbert Lyman had invited me to join him. I say "invited" because although I paid for my lodging, breakfast and midday dinner, he paid everything else for both of us, our way of living being entirely beyond the means of a student on half a Fellowship. We took a daily German lesson, and a daily walk; and in the evening, or rather in the afternoon—for the performances began at five or half-past five o'clock—we went to the Royal Theatre, hearing an opera or a play on alternate nights. The play often was Shakespeare, in the excellent German version. I remember *Julius Cæsar* particularly, a play that is not often done in English, I suppose because it is hardly a play for a star, like *Hamlet* or *Othello;* but the dutiful German State Company performed it with zeal and good judgment. We had an ample feast of Wagner, with Gudehus and Malten: old stand-bys but still adequate, singing and acting with a devout enthusiasm that was contagious. And after the theatre we had another treat that must not go unrecorded: an enormous delicious sweet omelette or *Pfannkuchen,* hot and crisp at the edges in its great pewter platter, followed by bread and cheese and a flagon of beer.

Memorable and important for me were these Dresden impressions: and I should include the lesson in architecture taught me by the Zwingler, the Royal Palace, and the Katholische Kirche; a lesson reinforced many years later by the monuments at Nancy. Baroque and rococo cannot be foreign to a Spaniard. They are profoundly congenial and Quixotic, suspended as it were between two contrary insights: that in the service of love and imagination nothing can be too lavish, too sublime, or too festive; yet that all this passion is a caprice, a farce, a contortion, a comedy of illusions.

All these wonderful things, besides the *Madonna di San Sisto* and everything else in the picture gallery, I saw while I stood side by side with Herbert Lyman, an intelligent observer who knew much more than I about music, yet a typical Yankee, cold, shrewd and spare inwardly, smiling with a sort of insulated incredulity at everything passionate, as if he lived inside a green glass bottle, warranted an absolute non-conductor. He condemned nothing, yet nothing seemed to make any difference *in him*. Why was he such a devoted friend of mine? We had no special interests in common, and I should not have distinguished him particularly from other kind and correct Bostonians if he had not shown such a marked and constant friendliness towards me. The secret of this was perhaps revealed by his younger sister one day at table in their house *in Beacon Street, opposite the Common*, the place where perfect Bostonians ought to live. The conversation had turned on summer resorts, and I said that I went every year to Europe, because the heat in New England was intolerable. This was tactless of me, since the Lymans had a luxurious ancestral house in Waltham near Boston which it would have been a crime for them not to occupy in summer, no matter what heat they might suffer there. However, I had smiled as I spoke, as if I couldn't really mean what I said. "Oh, thank you," cried the younger Miss Lyman, "we can't say that ourselves, but it's such a relief to hear it!" I expect that I said a good many things that it was a relief for her brother to hear. I was an exciting, slightly dangerous friend, yet not exactly disreputable, since I was by way of becoming a professor at Harvard. I could be acknowledged and cultivated and invited to the house. Moreover I had Bostonian connections. My sister was an intimate friend of Miss Sara Lowell, Herbert Lyman's own aunt, his mother's sister! Possibly he had heard of me before he had seen me, and that made such a difference in Boston! If my half-foreign sister was all right, why shouldn't I, at least educated in Boston, be all right also? He had very simple tastes; he liked my comic verses and would sing them to popular airs; for silly as the words were they could be sung without offence in any drawing-room. Yes, the partiality of the excellent Herbert for me was explicable. Other Bostonians, though they might not share it, could understand it. I was such a relief!

He not only sang a little, but would have liked to devote himself entirely to music. How, in what capacity? As a composer, as a performer, or merely as a critic, like "Billy" Apthorp in the *Boston Transcript*? Music would be an acceptable profession if you could begin by being famous. It was not acceptable if you were to begin at the foot of the ladder, and perhaps remain there. Herbert, who hadn't a great voice or a precocious talent, must therefore go into business. Yet there was no hurry about it. He might go to Germany for a year or two and study music. He would enjoy the Boston Symphony concerts all the more intensely every Saturday evening for the rest of his life. And his German musical holiday might well begin at Dresden. Now I was going to Germany too, where term at the universities didn't begin until the middle of November. Why shouldn't I spend the interval at Dresden? We could then learn German together, and have a good time as well. We had a very good time, but I, at least, didn't learn much German; I learned only what sufficed for my secret purpose—secret I mean even to myself. The purpose on which my heart was naturally set. This was not at all to be proficient in languages or to be a professor of philosophy, but to see and to understand the world. For this purpose our month or six weeks in Dresden was not merely a good preparation. It was a culminating point, one of the happiest episodes in my whole life.

I used at that time to sum up my first impressions of Germany by saying that there were three good things there: the uniforms, the music, and the beer. The formula was playful, yet it might still serve to express my sentiments if its terms were taken symbolically. *Uniforms*—which at that time were ornate and many-coloured, some sky-blue and silver, others white and gold—would stand for discipline and the glory of discipline. *Music* would stand for idealism, understood to mean love of ideal and immaterial things, of pure science and free imagination, and not "idealism" about material things, concealing or falsifying the truth about them. Finally *Beer* would stand for *Gemütlichkeit*, for joy in hearty, fleshly, kindly, homely, droll little things. How very much these three German virtues, when not exaggerated into vices, redeem the human soul from disorder, from servitude, and from spleen!

Berlin after Dresden seemed big, modern and ugly; but modernness, ugliness and bigness were familiar to me. I could live my own life in the midst of them, and so I did here. There were morning lectures with an interval of an hour between them: which I spent at the Museum, or at the Café Bauer over the English papers and a coffee with whipped cream. There was then a full dinner at half past one o'clock, in a restaurant upstairs near the Friedrichstrasse. It was so copious that, although this was my only solid meal, I usually skipped the boiled meat and vegetables, contenting myself with soup, fish, roast meat with vegetables, compote, and salad, and a dessert; washed down with half-bottle of white wine. The whole expense was three marks, two for the dinner, fifty pfennig for the wine, twenty-five for the coffee and the same for the waiter. I always sat at the same table, being one of the first to arrive, was expected, well received, and came to feel quite at home. I had a small room up many flights in the Louisenplatz, with a porcelain stove like a tomb in which a few diminutive cubes of synthetic fuel were buried every twenty-four hours. They did not make the room warm, but kept it from being too cold to sit in, warmly dressed, with a rug over one's legs. My landlady supplied coffee and rolls in the morning, and bread and cheese with a bottle of beer in the evening: so that after a good walk in the Thiergarten I would go home and devote the rest of the day and evening to work, without fear of interruption. At lectures I often sat with Strong, and sometimes with Houghton: they were my only acquaintances that year.

Of the four professors to whom I listened Paulsen was the

most important, not in himself—he was simply an excellent professor—but important for me as a medium and as a model of judicious and sympathetic criticism. This semester he lectured on Greek Ethics and in the next winter semester on Spinoza. In both subjects he helped to settle my opinions for good. The Greek ethics wonderfully supplied that which was absent in Spinoza, a virile, military, organic view of human life, a civilised view, to keep the cosmic and religious imagination of Spinoza in its proper moral place. The Greeks knew what it was to have a country, a native religion, a beautiful noble way of living, to be defended to the death. They recognised heroically that which Spinoza recognised only descriptively or pietistically: that the power of nature infinitely exceeds and ultimately destroys the power of each of its parts. The Greeks were thereby saved from arrogance without condemning themselves to littleness. For what is greater than beauty, and what is more beautiful than courage to live and to die freely, in one's chosen way? The Jews, on the contrary, and even Spinoza with them, fell into both littleness and arrogance: into the littleness of being content with anything, with small gains and private safety; and into arrogance in proclaiming that, in their littleness they possessed the highest good, heard the voice of absolute truth, and were the favourites of heaven. Undoubtedly if you renounce everything you are master of everything in an ideal sense, since nothing can disturb you: but the Jews never renounced anything that was within reach; and it was rather the Greek hero who renounced half of what he might have possessed, in order that the other half should be perfect.

I was thus fully settled in my naturalist convictions; they revealed the real background, the true and safe foundation, for human courage, human reason, and human imagination. These might, then, fill the foreground *ad libitum* with their creations, political and poetic. Both the Greeks and Spinoza, by a spontaneous agreement, combined the two insights that for me were essential: naturalism as to the origin and history of mankind, and fidelity, in moral sentiment, to the inspiration of reason, by which the human mind conceives truth and eternity, and participates in them ideally.

Besides Paulsen I heard Ebbinghaus who even asked me to his house, showed me his first fat baby and talked about William James, of course eulogistically, but with fundamental reservations, as for instance, on the question of freewill and responsibility, on which he said *"Das hat er eigentlich nicht durchgedacht."* This seemed rather a scholastic judgment to pass on James. He had thought and thought on that subject, yet he hadn't thought himself out of his half impulsive, half traditional horror of determinism, not because he couldn't think the argument out, but because, like Bergson, he didn't trust argument where he had intuition. Of course Ebbinghaus, whose training was scientific, knew that intuition is not a guide to matters of fact. James, however, was no draught-horse patiently pulling the scientific barge along a placid academic canal; rather a Red Indian shooting the rapids with spasmodic skill and elemental emotions. To Ebbinghaus it seemed that a professor's business was to trudge along the governmental towpath with a legal cargo, and I agreed with him technically much more than with James; but he was less interesting as a man and less challenging as a thinker.

I don't know for what reason I heard some lectures and took a seminar of Gezycki's—doubtless some recommendation from America, because Gezycki, who was a cripple, evoked emotional sympathies in reforming and free religious quarters in the Anglo-Saxon world. He defended English ethics rather than explained them; and his seminar on Kant's *Critique of Practical Reason* had no historical or critical value, but merely the interest of a pathetic personal cult of human happiness clung to passionately by an unhappy man. He too spoke to me of William James and of William James's brother-in-law Salter, who was a lecturer for the Ethical Culture Society. He was interested in James on the moral side, yet without spiritualistic leanings; and perhaps I may have learned from Gezycki to see that it is not *moral* to be romantic. This fact, for Gezycki, refuted romanticism; but for me it merely proves that the afflatus of romanticism belongs to the gnostic religions. It is a vital impulse expressed in fantastic assertions about the world; not (what Gezycki's heart desired) a social and personal discipline scientifically warranted to increase human happiness and abolish suffering.

For me, at that time, all this was of little account. What counted was Greek ethics, summed up in the stories that Herodotus tells about Solon, explaining the nature of happiness to the benighted Croesus. A string of excited, fugitive, miscellaneous pleasures is not happiness; happiness resides in imaginative reflection and judgment, when the *picture* of one's life, or of human life, as it truly has been or is, satisfies the will, and is gladly accepted. Epicurus had a different notion of happiness from that of Solon, but it was just as much a form of wisdom, a choice among possible lives; in neither sage was it a calculus of quantitative pleasures and pains. Epicurus renounced most of the things called pleasures, for the sake of peace, equanimity, and intelligence, and Solon's heroes renounced life itself for the sake of a beautiful moment or a beautiful death. The extreme of classical heroism here becomes romantic; because the most romantic career, if deliberately chosen and accepted without illusion, would be a form of happiness: something in which a living will recognised its fulfilment and found its peace.

After that first semester the wind was taken out of my sails for study in Germany. Strong and I had gone to England for the holidays; but I stayed at Oxford, and he joined other friends in Paris, neither of us returning to Berlin for the second semester. This was not dereliction on our part: we both had something better to do. Why hadn't someone warned us not to go to Berlin, but to choose some smaller place where there might be more unity of spirit in the teaching and in student life? Was there no such place at that unlucky moment? Were there no inspired philosophers then in Germany? Was there no enthusiastic romanticism and no *Gemütlichkeit*? For me it was a source of eternal regret to have missed the enrichment and the lesson that fusion with

German life, in my youth, might have given me. Nobody gave me clear advice in the matter, nor did Strong, who needed it less, seem to have received it, or to feel the danger we ran of wasting our time. He gave up the Fellowship for private reasons, and I, to whom it was then assigned, knew of nothing to do but to return to Berlin. All was changed there for me. Instead of keen curiosity and expectation, instead of delight at the freedom of thought and breadth of sympathy shown by my new professors, I was absorbed in other impressions and attachments. I had found England infinitely more interesting and stimulating than Germany. I had been again in Spain, even to Gibraltar, to receive my sister and had left her at my father's in Avila. I see now that I ought to have made a fresh plunge, a bold decision, gone to Marburg or Jena or Heidelberg or Bonn, seen only Germans, compelled myself to master the language, and lived, as during my first semester, an austere poor student's life.

At the time, however, I was will-less. Beal persuaded me to go to the pension, kept by an Englishwoman, where he was living, and where everyone was English or American. Mechanically I went again to hear the same professors. Paulsen was lecturing on Spinoza: a great treat, but essentially not a new light. I dropped in to listen to other lecturers occasionally, in their public courses: Wagner on political economy, Lasson on Fichte, Deussen on Schopenhauer and the Indians. I took a course under Simmel on *Ten Different Interpretations of the Essence of Kant's Critique of Pure Reason;* a clever series of criticisms, producing at least in my mind nothing but amusement and confusion. I was living in Babel. I felt no special inspiration, no guiding purpose, except the engagement involved in holding the Fellowship. Not that inwardly my devotion to philosophy was impaired. It remained my one all-embracing interest, not indeed as a science, only as a balance of mind and temper, in which all the sciences and arts should compose as true a picture as possible of nature and human nature. My quandary was not inward, it didn't concern my philosophy; it concerned only my academic position and possible

career. And from that point of view this German experiment
had been a failure. I was wholly incapable of taking a Doctor's
degree in Germany. The only thing for me to do was to return
to Harvard and take my Doctor's degree there, where I was at
home and sure of my ground. I knew German enough to write
my thesis on a German subject, if I might write it in English.
Then, unless a place as teacher were offered me somewhere—I
hardly thought of Harvard itself—I could go to the Institute of
Technology and study architecture.

I wrote to the Harvard authorities explaining my position, saying I was coming back, and asking to have my Fellowship renewed
as for a resident graduate. There was some hesitation about this
point, but in the end I got the appointment. It was not materially
indispensable to me, as I meant to live at my mother's in any
case, but gave me more leeway. I began that year to save, and to
possess a little capital. In other words, I began to prepare for
my retirement from teaching before I had begun to teach.

From ten to twenty years later I made several holiday visits
to Germany. They were in part acts of contrition for my youthful
waste of opportunities, yet I should hardly have made them
simply with that idea. The last of these visits I called a Goethe
pilgrimage, because I went expressly to Frankfort and to Weimar
to visit the home of Goethe's childhood and that of his old age.
I was then preparing my lectures on *Three Philosophical Poets*
of whom Goethe was to be one. Even that, however, would probably not have induced me to revisit Germany had I not meantime
formed a real friendship with a young German, Baron Albert
von Westenholz.

Westenholz was one of my truest friends. Personal affection
and intellectual sympathies were better balanced and fused between him and me than between me and any other person. I made
three trips to Hamburg expressly to see him, and he once joined
me in London and again at Amsterdam and in Brussels; but
travelling ultimately became impracticable for him, on account of
his health and hobbies, and I could never persuade him to come

to Italy, where we should have found so many themes for enthusiastic discussion. But we carried on a desultory correspond-
ence, and he never lost his interest in my philosophy and in my
books. Not that he was in any sense my disciple or surrendered
his independence of judgment. His liberal Lutheran background
and many-sided studies gave him independent points of view, and
his attainments were in many ways wider than mine; so that,
for instance, when in the later years I began to read New Testa-
ment criticism, chiefly in Loisy, he guided me very usefully to
various German authorities on the subject. He always maintained
an "Evangelical" conception of Christ very different from mine,
which is Gnostic and free from all claims to be historical. He
was too dutifully *gebildet*, too indoctrinated, to be as sceptical as
I am; and that difference lent spice to our discussions, especially
as he, with his lingering illusions, was the younger man and I, the
mentor, was the cynic. When my young friends are "gooder" than
I, I respect and love them, but when they are less tender than I
towards tradition, I feel that they are uneducated and stupid. I
could never accuse Westenholz of being stupid or uneducated:
but I felt to the end how *German* he was, how immersed in
learning and inclined to follow a sect, without much capacity
for laughter.

His father had been a partner in a family banking house established in Frankfort and Vienna, originally perhaps Jewish: but
my friend's mother was the daughter of a burgomaster of Hamburg, with the most pronounced Hanseatic Lutheran traditions.
The bank had a branch in London, and young Westenholz had
served his apprenticeship there and learned to speak English perfectly. But he never entered the firm: his health was far from
good: he suffered from various forms of mental or half mental
derangement, sleeplessness, and obsessions, which, however, he
himself diagnosed with perfect scientific intelligence. By way of a
rest-cure, he was sent on long ocean voyages; was wrecked off the
coast of Brazil, and later turned up at Harvard where he was
brought to see me.

I was then, in 1900–1905, living at No. 60 Brattle Street, and had my walls covered with Arundel prints. These were the starting point for our first warm conversations. I saw at once that he was immensely educated and enthusiastic, and at the same time innocence personified; and he found me sufficiently responsive to his ardent views of history, poetry, religion and politics. He was very respectful, on account of my age and my professorship; and always continued to call me *lieber Professor* or *Professorchen*; but he would have made a much better professor than I, being far more assiduous in reading up all sorts of subjects and consulting expert authorities. Before he left Cambridge, it was decided that I should visit him in Hamburg: I was to stay for a night at their town mansion (in an extensive park facing the Alster) to pay my respects to his invalid mother and his sister—a good many years older than he; and then he would carry me off to a little hermitage he had for himself in the woods, absolutely solitary, without even a carriage-road leading up to it.

Hamburg was not an inconvenient place for me to reach, since in those days I often sailed in the Hamburg steamers because they were the first to have single cabins, deep in the centre of the vessel, and well ventilated, so that I could hope to avoid seasickness, and to enjoy privacy. With these things secured, I was glad of a longish voyage, and instead of landing at Cherbourg or Southampton, I could easily go on to Cuxhaven and Hamburg: and the same convenience naturally existed for the return voyage. Our friendship became intellectually closer in later years, without seeming to require personal contacts; and I never went to Germany again after those external conveniences ceased to make the journey easy and as it were optional.

As for him, his impediments were growing upon him. Fear of noise kept him awake, lest some sound should awake him; and he carried great thick curtains in his luggage to hang up on the windows and doors of his hotel bedrooms. At Volksdorf, his country hermitage, the floors were all covered with rubber matting, to deaden the footfalls of possible guests; and he would run down repeatedly, after having gone to bed, to make sure that he had locked the piano; because otherwise a burglar might come in and wake him up by sitting down to play on it! When I suggested that he might get over this absurd idea by simply defying it, and repeating to himself how utterly absurd it was, he admitted that he might succeed in overcoming it; but then he would develop some other obsession instead. It was hopeless: and all his intelligence and all his doctors and psychiatrists were not able to cure him. In his last days, as his friend Reichhardt told me, the great obsession was with bedding: he would spend half the night arranging and rearranging mattresses, pillows, blankets and sheets, for fear that he might not be able to sleep comfortably. And if ever he forgot this terrible problem, his mind would run over the more real and no less haunting difficulties involved in money matters. The curse was not that he lacked money, but that he had it, and must give an account of it to the Government as well as to God. And there were endless complications; for he was legally a Swiss citizen, and had funds in Switzerland, partly declared and partly secret, on which to pay taxes both in Switzerland and in Germany; and for years he had the burden of the house and park in Hamburg, gradually requisitioned by the city government, until finally he got rid of them, and went to live far north, in Holstein, with thoughts of perhaps migrating to Denmark. A nest of difficulties, a swarm of insoluble problems making life hideous, without counting the gnawing worm of religious uncertainty and scientific confusion.

The marvel was that with all these morbid preoccupations filling his days and nights Westenholz retained to the last his speculative freedom. Everything interested him, he could be just and even enthusiastic about impersonal things. I profited by this survival of clearness in his thought: he rejoiced in my philosophy, even if he could not assimilate it or live by it: but the mere idea of such a synthesis delighted him, and my *Realm of Truth* in particular aroused his intellectual enthusiasm. In his confusion he saw the possibility of clearness, and as his friend Reichhardt said, he became sympathetically *hell begeistert,* filled with inspired light.

If this cohabitation of profound moral troubles with speculative earnestness was characteristically German, so was the cohabitation of both with childish simplicity. I was told one morning that that day was Fräulein Mathilde's thirty-third birthday. Where should I go to get some flowers or bon-bons to offer her with my congratulations: embarrassed congratulations, because if she had completed another year of life and that were so much to the good, it was less so that she had already completed thirty-three of them. But no: it was Sunday, and all shops were closed. I was genuinely sorry, because I am naturally remiss at paying compliments and attentions and giving due presents, and when an occasion presents itself boldly, I am glad to be forced to do the right thing. "If you really want to give her a pleasant surprise, write her a birthday poem," said Westenholz, seeing my perplexity. So I retired for an hour to my room and produced some verses, in which I congratulated the poor, the Baroness, Albert, and their friends on the prospect of having the *good* Mathilde (for she wasn't beautiful) with them for another year. The verses were worthless, but they had enough foundation in truth to serve their purpose. Mathilde really was all goodness, as Albert was too, only that he had intellect and madness to complicate the goodness.

In the afternoon, after a solid early dinner at which the Baroness was wheeled in a hospital litter to the table (for she insisted that she was too ill to sit up), brother and sister put their heads together to decide how they should celebrate the occasion; and it was decided that we three should go to their old house in the city, and take the dolls and the doll-furniture out of the boxes, and arrange everything in the dolls' house just as it used to be. Their old house was that of their maternal grandfather, who had been Burgomaster of Hamburg, belonging now to an uncle who wasn't living there for the moment. It was in the old town, near one of the churches with a high green steeple, and itself lofty and gabled: but we hurried up many flights of stairs as if treading on

forbidden ground: I should have liked to see the rooms, but foresaw difficulties in opening windows and conciliating caretakers
that would be involved in a visit of inspection unauthorised by
the owner: so that I too hurried guilty-like to the garret, under a
vast pitched roof, where evidently we might forget that we were
interlopers. The boxes were opened; the dolls, the furniture, the
crockery, were all distributed among the rooms of the immense
dolls' house, each precisely where it belonged. The names of the
various dolls were recalled, and in rapid German that I wasn't
expected to listen to sundry comic incidents of childhood were
referred to and enjoyed for the hundredth time. Then, dutifully,
everything was buried again in the boxes, to be resurrected perhaps when Fräulein's thirty-three years should have become forty-
five.

This joy in simplicity, this nostalgia for childishness, in highly
educated, rich, and terribly virtuous people surely is thoroughly
German: and doesn't it make some radical false turn, some organic
impediment, in their history? But let me not generalise. Westenholz at any rate was avowedly morbid and abnormal; without
being deformed, he had all the pathos and intensity that go
with deformity; jealousy and vanity, in professing to judge and
to dominate everything from above; great intellectual ardour and
display of theory; with genuine delight in the simplest pleasures
beneath, and temptation to the crudest vices. It would be a false
diagnosis to call him an old child, a pedant whose brain had
grown like a pumpkin, and left the heart rudimentary. His heart
was not rudimentary, it was large and nobly developed; but the
intellectual life accompanying it was not developed out of it but
borrowed, foreign, imposed by alien circumstances and traditions;
and for this reason, there was relief and joy in reverting from it to
homely things. *Los von Rom* is a very different cry in Germany
from what *No popery* was in England. In England, the King, the
prelates and the nobles felt ripe to be their own popes. They
wished to graft their culture on their instincts, and their instincts
were mature enough to breed a native culture, admirable in those

matters that touched English life—the home, the feelings, sports, politics, and manners, trade also and colonial conquests; yet their instincts were crude and incoherent in speculative directions, precisely in proportion as they receded from the manly arts of the native man. But in Germany the expression of the native heart had remained rustic and violent; *los von Rom* was a disruptive cry, expressing in enthusiasts an anarchistic impulse, and a rebellion against all control; whereas the princes and theologians and learned men who restrained that rebellion, and imposed a strict discipline on the people, imposed something alien and artificial, imposed officialdom, pedantry, or insane vanity. The heart might be free from Rome, but was enslaved to something far poorer and more acrid: so that a return to the heart became a reversion to childhood or to rusticity.

CHAPTER II

LONDON

THE GERMANY of 1886 had liberated, it had not enamoured me: and at the age of twenty-three a young man needs to be enamoured. A siren, however, was not far off, across the North Sea. After our first semester at Berlin, Strong and I decided to spend our holiday in England, and took ship at Bremen for London. It was a nasty voyage in a smallish German Lloyd steamer, an excellent cathartic to clear away all obstructions and leave a clean and keen appetite for something new. Regarding England I had favourable preconceptions derived from my father. It was in his opinion the leading country, the model country, for the modern world; and although this eminence might be patriotically claimed by Americans for America, it was not yet possessed by their country even in material things of importance; while in literature and philosophy, as well as in the art of living, the autarchy of the New World was that of the log-cabin: you might like roughing it and camping in the woods, but that did not create a new civilisation.

In approaching England I felt the excitement of a child at the play, before the curtain rises. I was about to open my eyes on a scene in one sense familiar from having heard and read so much about it. There was keen intellectual curiosity to discover the fact and compare it with my anticipations. There was my youthful hunger, still unappeased, for architectural effects, and picturesque scenes in general; and there was a more recent interest, destined to grow gradually stronger, in discovering and understanding human types, original or charming persons. And where were these more likely to be found than in England?

On our second evening from Bremen we had anchored in the

Thames and were to go ashore at Tilbury in the morning. Meanwhile, the customs officers came aboard to examine our papers and our luggage. We were almost the only first-class passengers; and it was without the least hurry, and almost in silence, that we laid our passports on the cabin table before the two quiet officials who had sat down there. Quiet they were, well spoken, laconic yet civil; half business-like and half deferential, as if in the first place they recognised us for gentlemen, and as if in general they were respectful towards other people's privacy and peace. Perfectly ordinary men like policemen; yet how different from any customs officials that I had ever come upon in Spain or America, in France or Germany! What *decent* officials! They didn't seem to suspect us of lying or cheating, and showed no tendency to brow-beat or deceive us with rigmarole and loudness. A national note, firmness beneath simplicity; a *decent* people, not very perceptive, a little stolid, decidedly limited, but sound, trained, running easily in the national harness. And this among the common people, when not misled. I was glad of this first impression; and it was curiously confirmed in my first journey to Oxford, in a third-class carriage. It happened to be full, five persons on a side, yet nobody said a word; or if any word passed from one to another, it was so brief, and so low in tone, as to disturb nobody else. Not genial, other nations might say, not friendly or human; but I felt that it was truly friendly, since it was considerate; it showed aptitude for getting on together, political aptitude, precisely because it let everyone alone, allowed them their place, and didn't blame them for existing even if their existence were a bit inconvenient.

So much for public manners, the best in the world; but soon I had a glimpse of the private feelings that might go with those manners in humble and ordinary people. We went to a boardinghouse that Strong had heard of in Notting Hill, a remote place for the sightseer, but correspondingly cheap and *decent*, besides having the incidental advantage of involving long drives on the top of busses, and often sitting (since we started at the start), only a little above and behind the driver's box, with whom a word might be exchanged occasionally, and whose powerful horses and skilful driving through the dense traffic might be admired. It was six miles, an hour's drive, to the Bank; and in that cool misty season with the sun high, but coppery and shining dubiously through the grey atmosphere, the swarming city, still moderately uniform in the character and the height of buildings, offered a scene of inexhaustible interest, justifying the humour of Dickens and Cruikshank, as well as the gentility of Thackeray. Everything seemed ready to be etched, from the broken-down old women in black bonnets selling matches at corners, to the black-and-white harmonies of St. Paul's and the churches in the Strand, poetic to see looming in the distance, and interesting to study on a nearer approach. Yet here doubts began to assail the mind, concerning the solidity of England in subtler matters of taste and allegiance, doubts confirmed by the then brand-new Law Courts. This Italian architecture of Wren's, this Ruskinian Gothic, were foreign here: they were whims, they were fashions, they were essentially shams. But the function of shams in English society is a large subject, and I shall revert to it often.

At table in Notting Hill one of the inevitable solitary elderly ladies explained to us how much they all loved Longfellow: he was a household poet in England no less than in America. I replied that I was not surprised to hear it; but that in America his vogue was beginning to pass away; at least we poets at Harvard never read anything written in America except our own compositions. As for English poets we admitted nobody less revolutionary than Swinburne or less pessimistic than Matthew Arnold. If the lady had been an American and younger she would have said I was horrid; being English and old she silently thought so, and merely repeated gently, that in England they loved Longfellow best.

There was also at table a modest, well-set-up young man, a clerk, who betrayed some interest in philosophy or, as I soon gathered, in religion. On that footing we became friends at once: I have always found it easy to form casual friendships, especially with

Englishmen. He said he belonged to the Church of the Apostles, commonly called Irvingites. Should I like to go to one of their services? Very much: and on the next Sunday he conducted me to a church like a Roman basilica, with an apse, quite orthodox mosaics, and a semi-circle of living apostles in stalls, wearing white smocks, and looking like a row of butchers, except that butchers seldom have long beards. The sermon informed us that it was not necessary to die. The Day of Judgment had long since come and people were constantly being caught up to heaven alive, perhaps as they walked in the streets, or through the chimney. My friend gave me no further evidence of this phenomenon; but I saw (which was what interested me) that for him these absurdities furnished a happy interlude in a drab life, a peep-hole into fairy-land, a little secret, unsuspected by the world, to keep up his self-respect, and cast a ray of supernatural hope into that small room in the third floor back, which might prove any day a jumping off place for a flight to heaven. By some chance his need of faith had attached him to the Irvingites; had his connections and education been more fortunate he might have become a high Anglican or Catholic; and his case showed, as it were under the microscope, the mechanism of conversion in higher spheres.

After two or three weeks at Notting Hill, spent in seeing everything in London that the guidebook recommended, Strong unexpectedly announced that he was obliged to join some family friends in Paris. He had evidently fresh money to spend, or was invited: I was not able or inclined to accompany him. Paris suggested a different side of life, and greater expenses; besides, I was intent on continuing my explorations in England and extending them at least to Oxford. Strong had dutifully kept me in the straight path of the earnest sightseer, visiting historic spots and notable monuments in the order of their importance and instructiveness, from the Tower to Madame Tussaud's. But when I was left alone, I began to live on a different plan, which I have followed when possible in all my wanderings. I moved to lodgings in Jermyn Street, Saint James's, No. 87, a house to which I was faithful for more than twenty-five years, and abandoned only bowing to *force majeure*. First Miss Bennett, the genial motherly landlady died: then her younger sister, a widow, married Colonel Sandys, who had long occupied the first floor. On arriving one year I noticed a change in the aspect of the house. The front door was painted a well-varnished dark green, with shining brass knocker and door-knobs; there was a fresh thick doormat, and when I rang the bell, though the man was the same familiar valet, he seemed much more spruce, and even a bit embarrassed in his conspicuously clean linen. The same lady, he explained, still lived here, but the house was no longer an hotel. And he politely presented me, on a solid silver tray, the letters that had arrived for me. There was nothing to do but to look foolish, and say, "Oh, indeed—I see—thank you," and get again into my taxi—it was already the age of taxis—and vaguely tell the driver to go somewhere else—anywhere—to the British Hotel a few doors beyond. But neither at the British Hotel nor elsewhere did I ever feel at home again in London lodgings; and this circumstance contributed to make my stay there always shorter and shorter.

Miss Bennett's was not a luxurious house, and I never took more than a single room there, and breakfast; yet though not a very profitable guest, I was a constant one, and always seemed to be welcome. I would even leave a hat-box there from year to year, as a sort of pledge, to get rid of the useless burden of a top-hat in the rest of my journeys. The full savour of the London of my youth, in the 1880's and 1890's, clings to my memories of Jermyn Street. I usually came down at nine or half-past to breakfast in a small back room on the ground-floor, always on bacon and eggs and *The Morning Post*. Sometimes another lodger would be there too but not often; and then we politely ignored each other's presence, concentrating each on his own teapot and toast-rack and dish of marmalade, and on his own newspaper, which in the other man's case was likely to be *The Times*. In the early days I preferred *The Standard,* because it was the Anglican clerical paper, opening to me the side of English life that interested me most; and when *The Standard* stopped publication, I took up *The Morning Post*, until that too succumbed—to the flood of vulgar journalism. After that I subscribed to no English newspaper; the continental press could inform me sufficiently about gross events, and I could always procure single copies of *The Times*, if there was anything of special importance.

The fire in Miss Bennett's breakfast room was the only common interest between the other lodger and me. Neither of us would attempt to monopolise it; we both kept at the distance that good form required. It would have been beneath us to huddle up close to it, as if we were ignominiously suffering from cold; yet we took good care not to retreat to such a distance as to abdicate the right to the best place, if we had come early and secured it. The best place then exalted the person who occupied it, and to preserve his Rights had become his Duty. I was being initiated into the secret of British politics.

In those days Jermyn Street preserved the character of a quiet and correct street in the heart of Saint James's. No. 87 was directly opposite the pleasant red-brick church with its pleasant trees, that made a green landmark, and with the pleasant broad face and pleasant chimes of its clock, that told you the hours. At night, lying warm in bed with the window open, I also liked to hear the patter, as of a child's drum, on the probably wet asphalt, as each hansom-cab, noiseless as to its wheels but *quadrupedante sonitu* as to its horse's hoofs, drove up the street, and drove away again in a brisk diminuendo.

It was precisely to the inveterate stranger in me that London had mightily appealed. All those hollow principles and self-indulgent whims of a decadent age had merged in the English gentleman into good form and sly humour; and in the Cockney they were reflected in his goodnatured derision and comfortable jollity. The spirit of London seemed remarkably mellow and rich in experience; for that very reason leisurely, gently mocking, not miscellaneously eager and hurried, like New York, nor false, cynical and covetous, like Paris. Not that great things have happened in

London; it has no such memories as Rome or Florence; but being a commercial city, a port and the centre of a colonial empire, it has encyclopedic contacts, and means of knowing the world at a distance without being very much disturbed by it in its own back-parlour. There is therefore balance in its omniscience, and a wise perspective in its interests. Experience fosters both affection and unconcern; and we are lucky when the affection settles down upon what is near, and the unconcern upon what is distant and irremediable, with a subtle amusement at both. This seemed to me to happen in the typical Londoner, and it made him an engaging person.

London has always responded to a rather youthful interest of mine, the interest in streets, in clothes, in manners, in curious architecture; also to my pleasure in casual acquaintances and small explorations. These human episodes enlivened the landscape and made particular spots memorable that would otherwise have been merged indistinguishably in the motley scene: yet it was the aerial landscape, always evanescent and always picturesque, that fed the spirit, as the cool moist air expanded the lungs. I loved the Parks—St. James's with its suggestions of by-gone fashions and a smaller town; Green Park, spacious and empty, like a country common; and Hyde Park above all, with its fashionable pedestrians and riders, its horses and carriages, and its band concerts; all easy to turn one's back on, for the sake of a long solitary walk. Yet these pleasures presupposed summer and fine weather. It was a setting for a holiday, not for a life. I never studied in London or read in the British Museum (as I did in the Bodleian) or gathered books, or made lasting friends. I visited nobody, not even the Sturgis connection: I was, and I liked to remain, an unrecognised wanderer.

Even the theatres seldom attracted me. British plays are ano-dyne, transparently moral or sentimental or intellectual; that is to say, not spontaneous products of the imagination. I think it must have been Protestantism that so completely extinguished Eliza-bethan genius. When the theatres were reopened at the Restoration, writers and audiences were utterly cut off from the healthy current of national life, and from the great classic and poetic tradition. They cared only for wit and satire and the evil pleasure of scandal. Now the wish to be edified has been added; but that limits the already slight range of the plays, without infusing into them anything poetical. The acting, too, is awkward and uninspired; the players are interested in themselves and not in their parts, and so are the audiences. Everything is modish, affected, trivial, and amateurish. Earlier, in the days of Irving and Terry, the stage production had been an object in itself. Elaborate scenery and costumes were designed to bring some historic epoch to light. Taste was preraphaelite; the stage resembled the Arundel prints after Pinturicchio that I had had in my rooms in Brattle Street. That fashion had passed when I was much in London, but the taste had not died in me, when the Russian ballet made its appearance. Here imagination and passion had fallen back upon first principles. Aestheticism had become absolute and violent, the appeal to the exotic and dream-like scorned to be accurate or instructive and was content to be vivid. Nor was elegance excluded, but it figured only as one *genre* among many, just as it does in Shakespeare and in real life. Delicacy was cultivated in its place, yet the way was left open in every direction to strength, to passion, to nature and to fancy. I wonder if Shakespeare could not be turned into Russian ballets to advantage: or into a kind of opera-ballet, in which the more important speeches could be introduced in recitative into the music. Aristophanes also might lend himself to such treatment.

It was only on rare evenings in London that I dressed or dined with friends or went to any show. I tasted the specific quality of the place better when I strolled about alone, dined in some grill room or in some restaurant in Soho, or walked out over the bridges to watch the evening glow reflected on the river. England preserves the softness and verdure of the country even in the city; and London, the densest of Babylons, is everywhere turned into a landscape by the mist, by the cloudracks, by the docks and ship-

ping towards the East, by the green reaches, the fields, the boating
crowds towards the West. It thins out and becomes rural imperceptibly in its immense suburbs, and not always vulgarly; there
are royal preserves and stately seats in all directions. Woolwich
steps down grandly to the sea, and Kensington Palace and Hampton Court lead nobly towards Windsor Castle. This instinct to
merge town and country in one limitless park, and never to lose
sight of a green field, an overhanging tree, or an impenetrable
hedgerow no doubt renounces architecture on the grand scale. The
city remains a conglomeration of accidents, of incongruous whims
and private rights huddled together. The roads turn and wind
round the freehold cottages and jealously fenced gardens, and
comfort is never sacrificed to symmetry. Yet in neglecting grandeur the Englishman remains jealous of his dignity, and also of
his privacy. He plants his neighbours out, if he possibly can; the
comforts he exacts are simple; too much luxury would be incompatible with quietness and liberty. Even in the great respect that
he shows for wealth and station he honours freedom rather than
power. Your rich man can do as he likes, and can live as he
chooses. Then the liberty that is a sham in public becomes a
reality in private.

To the classic mind landscapes are always landscapes with
figures. Even the desert, the sea, or the stars draw all their magic
from the solitude or sacred companionship that the soul feels in
their presence. So the aspects of a town borrow their quality from
the life that they suggest—market, temple, fortress, or garden.
London is essentially a commercial city. Everything about it hangs
upon that fact, even the golden mist and the black fog that makes
its beauty and its monstrosity; for they are effects of occupying
a watery place near the corner of an island; ideal for shipping
and in the midst of sea routes, and of being able at the same time
to burn prodigious quantities of soft coal. Civilisations and towns
created by commerce may grow indefinitely, since they feed on
a toll levied on everything transportable; yet they are secondary.
However much they may collect and exhibit the riches of the

world they will not breed anything original. Their individuality and excellence, no less in Venice than in London, will be the fruit of accidents, of converging influences and borrowed traditions. If an Englishman set out to be a *great* man, a genius, a saint, or a responsible monarch, the devil would soon pocket him. It is only the rich Englishman that can truly prosper in England. Like the Lord Mayor of London, he can dress up in a traditional costume, and receive Royalty and all other grand people at his feasts. He can repeat the consecrated platitudes, and drink the approved wines; and in his hours of obscurity and thrift, labor; he can revise accounts, poke his library fire, drink tea with his buxom wife, and send his sons to Eton or Harrow. Commercial communities in this way accumulate great treasures and hand down admirable institutions; yet in them the whole exists only for the sake of the parts and their greatness is only littleness multiplied. They become museums, immense hostelries, perpetual fairs. Society will be nowhere brisker or more various. Everything that money can buy will be at the command of those that have money. The dandies and snobs will lead the aristocracy; fashion will nowhere be more splendid and more respected, and misery nowhere more squalid. The metropolis will overflow with life gathered from the four quarters of the heavens; it will never be a fountain of life.

As to the fish swimming about in this whirlpool, I could infer from my American experience of a society even more commercial and casual, that they had individual souls and personal histories; and I had learned in Dickens something about such souls in the lower classes, the Sam Wellers and the Mrs. Gamps, and among the merchants and lawyers, for whom London was all in all. These are not classes in which a stray foreigner like me would be likely to make acquaintances; and a metropolis is not like a ship or a college, where prolonged contact with the same persons discloses their individualities even to the least sympathetic stranger. Yet in the classes with which intercourse was easier for me, I did pick up various acquaintances; and some of those figures have remained pleasantly painted in my memory.

One day in Jermyn Street, when I had breakfasted in bed and came down nicely dressed about noon, fat Miss Bennett, who was arranging the flowers in a row of little vases in the narrow entry, smiled in her motherly way as she made room for me to pass, and said, "You have been doing the young lady this morning, Sir." Yes; though I was no longer a young man (this was in 1901) I had had a momentary lapse into fashionable life, and was going to take a turn in the Park before lunching at Hatchett's; and I confided to her that the previous evening I had been dining at the Savoy with two young officers of the Guards. It had been as far as possible from a debauch—I will describe it presently—but it had thrown me back into the mood of 1897, when I had known a knot of young men about town, acquaintances made at Cambridge; not all English, for there was an Australian and a Frenchman, and for that reason all the more knowing and entertaining. At that time (in my holiday year at King's and in Italy) I had been wide awake; but now I had entered a somnambulist tunnel, where the engines worked and the wheels made a more furious noise than ever, but where the spirit was suspended on the thought: When shall we come out again into the light and air? The two Guardsmen brought a glimpse into the open, not promising but suggestive. They knew nobody in my world, I knew nobody in theirs. Yet I, at least, was never more in my element than when I was far from myself. How did I know them?

We were waiting on the pier at Southampton in the previous September for the German liner that was to convey us to America. Fog had kept her from making the port on time. In standing about the steamer-office, waiting for information, I noticed two young Englishmen, well dressed, good-naturedly accepting the accident of being sent to dine and to spend the night at a local hotel, and being correspondingly delayed in their arrival in New York. They evidently didn't care. They were not going to America on business: I wondered what they were going for. For nothing, perhaps, to spend the time, to see the Rocky Mountains, or to look for heiresses. There was an air about them of being thoroughly equipped, perfectly trained and hardened, thoroughly competent to do anything and not knowing what on earth to do.

The next day on board, when the chief steward had found a place for me in the dining-room, there were the two young men, directly opposite me at the same table. Their casual conversation was not audible to me: they were English. After a day or two, however, in passing the mustard or the salt, we began to exchange a few phrases, and gradually came to joining forces on deck or in the smoking-room. The smoking-room was my place of refuge in transatlantic steamers, when I was not walking on the lower deck, which was clear of chairs, nearer the water, and comparatively deserted, allowing freedom of movement as well as of mind. When I had taken my exercise, and wished to sit down, I looked for a comfortable corner in the smoking-room. The smoking-room was the one place sure to be well ventilated; there were deep leather chairs where I could read at ease or even write in a note-book. The crowd and the hubbub didn't in the least disturb me, since I wasn't asked to attend to it. Here I could have tea, and here sometimes my two new friends would join me, and would explain incidentally they were simply on a tour, curious about America and apparently entertained by what I said of it. They were eventually coming to Boston, and I rashly offered to show them the sights of Harvard.

Rashly, I say, because when they turned up a month or two later, it puzzled me to think what the sights of Harvard were. These young men didn't want to see the stadium (then a novelty) nor the glass flowers. The Yard was leafless, muddy and at its ugliest, and I no longer lived there but in Brattle Street, not in rooms worth showing. Nor had I any longer any interesting friends that I could have asked to meet them at tea. So I frankly confessed my predicament and took them to see Memorial Hall with the panorama (and smell) of a hundred tables and a thousand men at dinner—for it was already six o'clock. They said it looked like Sandhurst. Evening had already come and there was nothing to do but to walk back to Main Street and to the electric car that would take them back to Boston. By way of apology for this futile afternoon, I sent two books to their ship to entertain them on their homeward voyage: my *Interpretations of Poetry and Religion,* then just out, for A, the one who seemed more intellectual, and Flandrau's *Diary of a Freshman* for the other, B, who was apparently simpler and younger. I knew that the first book was too serious and the second too frivolous, but perhaps between them they might represent the winds blowing at Harvard.

When I dined with them the next summer in London, I felt that they had asked me to the Savoy because they were in much the same predicament that I had been when I took them to the gallery of Memorial Hall: they wanted to be civil to me, but they had to invent a way. The food was excellent—all cold, by a caprice of B's—and they spied well-known people at some other tables, whose names they whispered with smiles: but they might have dined more pleasantly and cheaply by themselves at the Guard's Club, to which strangers were not admitted. The evening was clear and they proposed walking back to Pall Mall, exactly what my instinct would have prompted me to do. This undercurrent of common tastes was what established pleasant relations between them and me, in spite of completely different backgrounds. When we reached Pall Mall, I knew they were making for their club; I therefore said good night and turned up through St. James's Square, reflecting on what a tax it is to entertain strangers, even for people enjoying every advantage in the heart of London. Besides, three, except among very intimate friends, is not a propitious number for conversation: it renders sympathies shy to show themselves and interesting subjects hard to follow up. To cement a new friendship, especially between foreigners or persons of a different social world, a spark with which both were secretly charged must fly from person to person, and cut across the accidents of place and time. No such spark had seemed to pass between these young men and me; and yet I was sure, especially in the case of B, that a latent sympathy existed unexpressed: and the proof of it appeared not many days later. B wrote asking me to dine with him again, without dressing, in the most singular of places for dining—in the Bank of England. He happened to be for the moment the officer commanding the guard at that place; and this officer had the privilege of inviting one person to dine with him, and of drinking one bottle of claret and one of port. Would I come?

It was raining hard on the appointed evening and when I told my cabby to go to the Bank—the Bank of England—the fellow almost laughed in my face, but in a moment recovered his professional gravity, and observed a bit quizzically, "Bank, Sir? Bank will be closed, Sir," evidently doubting whether I was a little mad, or excessively green. I said I knew it was closed to the public, but went there by special appointment; and I jumped in resolutely, and closed the doors. My man started, driving at first rather slowly, but being once in for it, gained courage, and drove smartly the rest of the way. When I had got out and paid him, I noticed that he lingered a moment. His curiosity wasn't satisfied, without seeing whether people ever got into the Bank of England at eight o'clock in the evening.

The policeman at the door, on the contrary, understood everything, said "This way, Sir," affably, and hurried me across the court faster than I could have wished, because the scene was wonderful. In those days the court you first entered was surrounded by pavilions no higher than the blank outer wall; various crosslights from archways, doors and windows were caught and reflected by the wet pavements and casual puddles, or lit up bright patches of scarlet or brass or shining white belts in the groups of soldiers, hard to distinguish under the black sky, who lounged in the doors or huddled for shelter under the eaves. I thought of Rembrandt's *Night Watch*; but this scene was more formless yet more alive. Here everything trembled, water trickled and sparkled over all; and in the darkness itself there was a sense of suspended animation among ambiguous shadows that would yield for a moment to recognisable reality, where a face lifted or an arm moved or a voice spoke some commonplace word.

The room into which I was ushered had a dingy Dickensian look of solidity grown old-fashioned and a bit shabby. There was a walnut mantelpiece with a small clock and two candlesticks without candles; heavy black walnut chairs, with horsehair bottoms, and a table set unpretentiously, with thick white plates and thick glasses. But there was a pleasant fire in the grate, and the rather superannuated butler served us an excellent absolutely English dinner: mock-turtle soup, boiled halibut with egg-sauce: roast mutton: gooseberry tart and cream, and anchovies on toast; together with the two bottles of wine already mentioned. Too much food, you might say; but in the English climate, distressing to the lazy but friendly to the active man, after a long day pacing the streets in rain and shine as if you were pacing a deck, all that food was appetising. The old butler knew that it was just right, whatever notions the young officers of to-day might have got into their heads. One had to put up with them; but he was conscious of the whole weight and authority of the Bank of England backing him up. Where would the Army be without the Bank? Nowhere.

The good claret and port were left entirely to me. My poor friend was under the doctor's care and could drink only milk. He seemed very young and very dejected, in his white flannel shirt and sporting jacket, while his red and gold tunic and his huge bearskin lay on a chair, waiting to be put on at eleven o'clock for the evening inspection, when I should have to leave. We had a friendly philosophic talk about the troubles of youth—the chief of them being that youth cannot last. This fatality casts its shadow before it and makes the young dissatisfied with youth, although what will follow will probably be no better. My two Guardsmen were apparently thinking of resigning their commissions; something that surprised me a little in the case of A who I knew had made a special study of gunnery. As for B, soldiering was what any obligation is for the vaguely young—a constraint with some compensations. He was bored in the Army; but the devil of it was, what to do afterwards. Pity he hadn't found an American heiress; he would have been quite happy as a country gentleman, with nice horses and nice children. Perhaps he would have preferred an English heiress, who wouldn't have wanted to rush back to New York every winter; or perhaps he was already in love with someone who was not an heiress, and who drove him to foolish adventures in the vain effort to forget her. I was sorry for the poor chap. Most enviable of men, I should have thought him, in his person and surroundings; yet for that very reason he seemed to have no future. The garden that had bred him, having seen him bloom, had no further use for him. It is indeed in the nature of existence to undermine its best products, and also its worst. This may be an acceptable reflection to the philosopher, who dwells in the eternal, but not for the fatted calf being led to the slaughter.

Our conversation was interrupted by a knock at the door. The sergeant came to report that one of the men had been taken ill. "Get a cab—a four-wheeler would be better"—my friend said thoughtfully, "take him to the barracks and bring back another man," and he gave the sergeant some money for the fares. "Doesn't the Government," I asked, "pay little items of this sort?" "Oh, I suppose I might charge it, but it's hardly worth while. It doesn't happen very often." He spoke in his habitual tone, half resignation, half amusement; but I suspected an impulse beneath to look after his men personally, and to let them feel that the imperturbable air of an officer didn't exclude a discerning good will towards his soldiers. The ethos of an aristocratic society, I perceived, is of a very high order. It involves imaginative sympathy with those who are not like oneself, loyalty, charity and self-knowledge.

It seemed a good moment to say good night, without waiting for the hour when I should be asked to leave. The rain had ceased; many of the lights in the court had been put out; the place seemed emptier and more ordinary than before. When the ponderous doors had been closed after me, I looked at my watch. It was half past ten. The pavement was wet, but I had on thick boots. Why not walk back the whole length of Fleet Street and the Strand? If I had melancholy thoughts, the cool moist air and the pleasant exercise would transform them. Scattered lights revealed only nebulous spaces, as the stars do in the sky, save where a few stragglers loitered in the glare of the theatre entrances. Morally all things are neutral in themselves. It is we that bathe them in whatever emotion may be passing through us. That singular evening at the Bank of England remains for me a picturesque image, lurid, cynical yet on the whole happy.

Thirteen years later, in July 1914, I was on my way for a short visit to England with a return ticket to Paris in my pocket, good for three months. As soon as I got into the boat at Calais, I prudently hastened to have a bite in the cabin before we left the dock; that, with a useful medicine that I had learned to take, would help me to weather the passage. I was having my cold meat and beer at one end of the empty table, when a steward came to ask me if I was Mr. Santayana—or something that represented that sound. The gentleman at the other end had sent him to inquire. I looked up, and in spite of astigmatism and near-sightedness in me and the ravages of ten years in him, I recognised my young Guardsman. I nodded assent to him, and immediately gulped down the rest of my beer and went over to say how-do-you-do. But I couldn't stop; he knew I was a bad sailor; and I must go and find a sheltered spot on deck. I would look for him there later, weather permitting, or in any case at Dover. Yet I didn't look for him: on the contrary I chose a nook on the lower deck, in the second-class portion, wrapped myself up in a great-coat and rug, and weathered the passage undisturbed and without accident. At Dover, however, I found him standing before the train that was to take us to Charing Cross. We exchanged a few words. He was going home, he said, to rejoin his regiment. He was with ladies. The ladies were already in the carriage, and looked as if they might be his mother and sister or his wife and mother-in-law. In any case, they would certainly prefer to travel by themselves, and I discreetly got into another compartment.

We had each other's addresses. Perhaps if I had known I was to remain in England for five years, or if he had known that he was to die in five months, it might have occurred to one of us to write; but neither of us did so. It was better not to force a renewal of our acquaintance. Our paths were divergent, neither of us was any longer young, and it had been his youth and that very divergence that for me had made our acquaintance interesting. There would no longer be anything strange in his being unhappy. He had lost his good looks and his mocking pleasure at the ways of the world. Although still a soldierly figure and distinguished, he was now yellow, battered and preoccupied. I rather suspect a wife and children didn't exist; if they did, his end, for them, may have been a tragedy. But for a bachelor tired of knocking about and doing nothing in particular, a gallant death was a solution. It placed him becomingly in the realm of truth and crowned the nonchalance of his boyhood.

It was on this trip, in July 1914, that I found 87 Jermyn Street, "no longer an hotel"; a trivial circumstance in itself that still marked the end of my pleasant days in London. I was there henceforth only on the wing, as at a centre from which to visit my friends in the country, or to go for a season to Oxford or Cambridge. I was at Cambridge, at the Red Lion, in the first days of that August, when war broke out; and I was again in London, at rooms I often took afterwards at 3 Ryder Street, when one evening, as I was going to bed, I heard a great crash. They must have dropped a heavy tray of dishes in the pantry, I thought: but presently came another crash very like the first, and then other detonations: it was the first Zeppelin raid. I put on again such clothes as I had taken off, and went down into the streets. It was not late, hardly eleven o'clock; and the people about were naturally excited and communicative. I went as far as Piccadilly Circus, from whence I could see, towards the east, the glare of distant fires. One corner shop in the Circus had been smashed: I suppose that was the first great noise that I had taken for broken crockery. The next evening many people waited late in Hyde Park, to see if there would be another raid; but nothing occurred. Nevertheless here was now another reason for not staying in town, and I soon moved to Oxford, favourably placed, from the point of view of safety, in the very middle of England, not yet an industrial town, and the proverbial seat of quietness, religion and study.

The moment when I lost my pleasure in London was the very moment when I was at last free and might have settled down there, as would be natural for an unattached man who writes in the English language. Moreover, unlike most foreigners, I was perfectly happy in the English climate and the English way of living. They were a great relief from America in softness and dignity, and from the Continent in comfort and privacy. Yet a somewhat mysterious contrary force prevented me from making the attempt. Perhaps it was my age. I was fifty, and the prospect backward had begun decidedly to gain on the prospect forward. For the future, I desired nothing fixed, no place in society, no circle of prescribed friends and engagements. Direct human relations, certainly, with whatever persons I might come across, which might include stray poets or philosophers, or agreeable ladies, for instance, like "Elisabeth." But they should come and go, and I should be free always to change the scene and to move into another sphere. For constant company I had enough, and too much, with myself. A routine had established itself in my day, which I could carry with me wherever I went; it gave me abundance of private hours, and for relief and refreshment, I liked solitude in crowds, meals in restaurants, walks in public parks, architectural rambles in noble cities. To have become simply an old bachelor in London would have been monotonous. Acquaintance with varied and distinguished people, which London might have afforded, didn't in the least tempt me. The intellectual world of my time alienated me intellectually. It was a Babel of false principles and blind cravings, a zoological garden of the mind, and I had no desire to be one of the beasts. I wished to remain a visitor, looking in at the cages. This could be better done by reading people's books than by frequenting their society.

With few exceptions, nobody of consequence in London knew of my existence. Even my publishers, except old Mr. Dent, remained unknown to me, as Scribner had remained unknown in New York. I can remember only one literary man that (through Loeser, I believe) became a sort of friend of mine: and then it was his wife rather than himself that was eventually well known to the international public: but my London friend was her husband, Arthur Strong. He was at that time librarian to the House of Lords and was believed to get up the facts for the speeches of the Prince of Wales, later King Edward VII. He had been originally librarian to the Duke of Devonshire, with whose house he was said to be somehow connected.

Mrs. Strong was a large woman, with bold pseudo-classic features like a late Roman statue of Niobe; and when I saw her in their house in London, she looked like a figure by Burne-Jones that had walked out of the canvas: great heavy eyes, a big nose, a short upper lip, and full, richly curving lips, over a conspicuous round chin. But the most characteristic thing about her was the neck, long, columnar, and extremely convex in the throat, as if she habitually yearned forwards and upwards at once. She was also, at that time, preraphaelite in dress. I remember her one day at luncheon in green cotton brocade, with a broad lace collar, like a bib drooping over it. She was silent, and let her husband talk. Perhaps her thoughts were far away from him and from me. She was destined to become a Catholic and an authority on the history of Christian art, especially Roman archeology of the early centuries: and when I came across her once at the Berensons' in Florence, she did not recognise me or seem to remember that I had several times been her guest in London.

With Arthur Strong's mind I felt a decided sympathy. He was very learned in important but remote matters, such as Arabic literature. His central but modest position in the great world gave him a satirical insight into affairs, and he summed up his inner solitude in pungent maxims. He reminded me of my father. Through the Moors he had good knowledge of Spain also: and he said something about the Spanish mind that has given me food for reflection. "The Spaniard," he said, "respects only one thing, and that is—", and he raised his forefinger, pointing to heaven. There is no power but Allah: he is omnificent, and all appearances and all wills are nought. It is quite true that no genuine or reflective person in Spain trusts anybody or is proud of himself. He may be vain and punctilious, but that is play-acting: he thinks that pose is set down for him in his rôle; but inwardly he knows that he is dust. This is the insight that I express by saying to myself that the only authority in existence is the *authority of things:* that since only *things* have any authority there is, *morally,* no authority at all, and the spirit is free in its affections. Is this what the Moslems really feel? At any rate something keeps them (and me) from hurrying and fussing and being surprised. It is better to put up with things than to be responsible for them. We may leave responsibility, like vengeance, to God who made us and made the world and seems not to be disturbed at the result.

There was another member of the intelligentsia in London with whom I sometimes discussed high subjects. Of late years he has explained himself very well in his memoirs, entitled *Unforgotten Years.* I came upon him from two sides: Bertie Russell had married one of his sisters, and Berenson eventually married the other. It was Bertie that first introduced me to the Smith family, Quakers from Philadelphia long resident in England. In the name of his parents-in-law he wrote asking me to come to Friday's Hill, a place they had taken in Haslemere. I went, and found myself in an odd society. Old Mr. Smith, prosperous and proprietor of a thriving factory, had been also a Quaker preacher, and no less successful in saving souls than in making money; but, alas, in the midst of his apostolate he had lost his faith, and was at a loss how to reply to his trustful converts when they came to him for further guidance along the narrow path. "Don't tell Mrs. Smith," he said to me while showing me his garden, "but I am not a Christian at all.

I am a Buddhist." And he pointed to what he called his Bo Tree, a great oak, in the midst of which he had had a glass house constructed. We climbed the ladder into it, a single small chamber with a black horsehair lounge and a small bookcase, filled with little old-fashioned American books, among which I spied *Prue and I,* a novel by our "Aunt Sarah's" son-in-law, George William Curtis. I had expected the Dhammapada or the Upanishads. Vain flight of the American puritan to softer climates! He carries his horizon with him, and remains rooted at home.

Mrs. Smith too had been a preacher, and she remained a Quaker inasmuch as she continued to advocate simplicity of life and to call her children "thee"; and although she had abandoned the belief in hell, she went on preaching and feeling the immense importance of rescuing oneself from perdition; for as she wisely thought, there were bad enough hells on earth from which people needed to be saved. However, with a resignation that had a touch of defiance and warning in it, she put up with the unregenerate views of her children, and of the world at large.

It was strange to see Bertie, and even his brother, who turned up one day for luncheon, in that American Quaker family, and to hear those young women speak of the elder brother as *Frank,* which I never heard any of his friends or his wives do. But the Russells never knew themselves or their proper place in the world: that was a part of their mixture of genius and folly. I myself felt out of my element in the Smith family, yet was destined to come upon them all my life long in various ways. They not unnaturally thought of me among their class of expatriate Americans and members of the intelligentsia: only Mrs. Berenson, who had motherly insights and had been married to an Irish Catholic, understood me a little, and perceived how unwillingly and deceptively I had come to fall under those categories. However, I have much to thank the Smiths for. They formed a lively band in the carnival, and led me into other bands in the masquerade, which I should hardly have joined of my own initiative.

At Haslemere, they took me to visit "Michael Field," whose

identity and whose poems I had never heard of. Michael Field was a pseudonym for two ladies, aunt and niece, who were linked together by the tenderest affection and by a common inspiration of the classic Muse. They had been forewarned, they may have read up my poetry expressly; in any case, they awaited me as if I had been Orpheus approaching lyre in hand towards their bower. The aunt stood at the door, serene but intense; dressed in rich black lace: I noticed a preciously bound small volume in her hand and pink roses in her bosom. The niece kept somewhat in the shadow, as if too young to be more than silent and curious. On the tea-table there were red and green apples in a golden basket, and under the table a large dog, with a wonderful coat of long silken bronze-coloured hair. Unfortunately the dog couldn't travel and would die if they left him: for that reason they were prevented from ever going to Italy and Greece. But what did that matter, when they had Greece and Italy in their hearts? They didn't say so in words, but words in such a case were superfluous. Everything breathed inexpressible tenderness and silent passion.

Some years later the Smiths introduced me to a better-known personage: Henry James. Bertie and his first wife had then been divorced and she and her brother lived together in St. Leonard's Terrace in Chelsea. By that time Logan Pearsall Smith had developed his amiable interest in my writings and the Berensons also had shown me the greatest kindness. Now the brother and sister asked me one day to lunch with Henry James. Those were his last years and I never saw him again. Nevertheless in that one interview he made me feel more at home and better understood than his brother William ever had done in the long years of our acquaintance. Henry was calm, he liked to see things as they are, and be free afterwards to imagine how they might have been. We talked about different countries as places of residence. He was of course subtle and bland, appreciative of all points of view, and amused at their limitations. He told me an anecdote about Prosper Mérimée wondering at him for choosing to live in England, and finding that a good background for his inspiration.

"Vous vivez," he had said, *"parmi des gens moins fins que vous."*
All of us naturally felt the truth of this as applied to Henry
James, and each of us no doubt thought it true of himself also:
yet how well we all understood, notwithstanding, the incom-
parable charm of living in England!

As for me, apart from the climate and the language, both
entirely to my taste, there was the refinement, if not the *finesse*
of English people in all their ways. They were certainly less
disinterested than I, intellectually, morally and materially; and it
was not from them that I wished to draw my ideas. But I respected and loved the English psyche, and the primacy there of
the physical and moral nature over the intellectual. It was the
safer order of things, more vital, more manly than the reverse.
Man was not made to understand the world, but to live in it. Yet
nature, in some of us, lets out her secret; it spoils the game, but it
associates us with her own impartiality. We cannot abdicate that
privilege. It is final, ultimate, proper for the funeral oration over
the earth: but those who are destined to live in this world had
better not hear of it, or if they hear of it had better not take it
too much to heart.

Of the London suburbs, the only one where I have stayed for
any time is Richmond. I saw the old Star and Garter at its last
gasp; it was being sold and transformed: and while the dinner
there was good enough, there was an uncomfortable air of removal.
But during the year of the armistice I spent some weeks at the
Richmond Hill Hotel; I was waiting to obtain leave to return to
Paris. The French authorities made a great fuss about it. Why, if
I had lived in Paris, had I abandoned *La France* in the hour of
danger? The military official evidently suspected that I was not a
neutral or an elderly man, but a young coward or a secret enemy.
I might have retorted that if I had returned at the outbreak of
war, I should only have added another mouth to the population,
quite likely to be starved during another siege. But I never protest or argue with persons in authority: instead I produced a note
in a fashionable lady's handwriting. It was from Madame de

Fontenay, addressed to the Chancellor of the French Embassy, requesting him to facilitate my journey, and including her husband's card. She wrote because I was a friend of the Strongs who were great friends of hers; and they were great friends of hers because they were son-in-law and granddaughter of Rockefeller. Monsieur Rockefeller, she once said to me with decision, was like a king. Her perfumed little letter worked like magic; and I was immediately able to cross the Channel; it was on the very day of the signing of the peace of Versailles.

In Richmond I had not had the comfort of private lodgings, but had quiet and rather nice early Victorian rooms; and for going in to London, as I did often, I liked the top of the busses, now motor-busses, and the long drive over Fulham Heath. On other days Richmond Park was at hand for walks in almost complete solitude. The Terrace, the tea-rooms, the river, and the trippers entertained me after the fashion of the Paris boulevards.

One day I fell into conversation with a young man who was reading a French novel conspicuous in its yellow cover. They all knew French and Italian, he said, in the Navy. He had cruised all over the Mediterranean. Now he was on special leave because his father was on his way to England to try the Kaiser. His father was a Chief Justice in India—Watkins: I had of course seen the name. Yes: I had certainly seen the name somewhere: I didn't add, over the fishmonger's round the corner. And the Chief Justice and his gallant son were enjoying their holiday for nothing. They didn't after all hang the Kaiser. Such little casual acquaintances amused me in my travels.

I had been in Richmond once before on a much briefer, soberer, more exalted errand: to visit old Lady Russell at Pembroke Lodge. Bertie took me there to high tea one evening. There was a beef-steak, and a half bottle of claret, exclusively for me. The atmosphere was exactly that of old-fashioned Boston: only the voices and the subjects of conversation were different. Lady Russell at once asked me if I knew *The Bible in Spain*. I had heard of Borrow's book, but unfortunately hadn't read it, so that I was at a loss to make a suitable reply. Soon, however, I was put at my ease by not being questioned, and Lady Russell—her daughter Lady Agatha was present but didn't talk—began to speak about herself and her feelings. The world had moved away from what it was in other days: she never went to London now except to dine with Mr. Gladstone. In fine, a picture of self-confirming but melancholy old age, when the nebula of experience contracts into a single central sun, alone now visible or trusted, and destined soon to be extinguished in its turn.

This visit forms an interesting contrast to the one, already mentioned, which I had made some years before to the Russells' other grandmother, Lady Stanley of Alderley. There I had been taken by the elder brother, here tabooed. I had just returned to London from Oxford, and Russell had asked me to join him at his grandmother's, on the way to Teddington, where he then lived. It was a large house in Dover Street, now a club or hotel. The front door, at one end of the façade, opened directly into a large square hall, where I was received by two flunkeys in white silk stockings. When I asked for Lord Russell and gave my name, it was evident that I was expected, for the footman I spoke to said, "Yes, Sir. In a moment," and the other instantly disappeared. Presently I saw the youthful figure of Russell himself tripping down the red carpeted grand stairs, and I can see it still, silhouetted against the western sunlight that streamed from the opposite windows above the landing. He was in an amiable mood, seemed to approve of my new clothes and hat and discreet tie, and led me up in the most friendly manner into a long room like a gallery that evidently occupied the whole front of the house. There was a row of windows, with boxes of plants in front of them, running along one side, and opposite a row of cabinets and sofas against the wall, the whole floor between being clear, and with the parquet highly burnished and waxed, so that footing was a bit precarious. At the other end, however, there was a large rug spread, on which stood the tea-table, surrounded by three ladies, and two or three vacant chairs of comfortable and homelike appearance. Lady Stanley, fat, old, jolly, and monumental, was enthroned in the centre; on one side sat the Hon. Maud Stanley, her daughter, amiable and middle-aged, and on the other her granddaughter, Lady Griselda Ogilvie, charming in the latest fashion and smiling with an easy grace. Our visit was as short as it was agreeable, for Russell was always conscious of the due time for catching trains. But it sufficed to leave a permanent impression in my mind, since this is the only glimpse I ever had of a grand house and of good society in London.

The recollection will serve to bring my rambling narrative back to the year 1887, and to the most extraordinary of all my friends.

CHAPTER III

RUSSELL

BECAUSE the windows of my room in Hollis Hall looked out directly on the brick path that led from the Harvard Yard to Jervis field, then the college playground; or because, for an undergraduate, I was thought comparatively articulate; or because I was a foreigner and known to write verses; or because the guide to whom the young Earl Russell was entrusted was a good friend of mine,[1] that exceptional nobleman, grandson and heir of Lord John Russell, was brought to see me, when on being "sent down" from Oxford in 1886 he visited America in charge of a tutor. He was the first Englishman I had ever spoken to or that had ever spoken to me. That of itself would have made him notable in my eyes; but this Englishman was remarkable on his own account.

He was a tall young man of twenty, still lithe though large of bone, with abundant tawny hair, clear little steel-blue eyes, and a florid complexion. He moved deliberately, gracefully, stealthily, like a tiger well fed and with a broad margin of leisure for choosing his prey. There was precision in his indolence; and mild as he seemed, he suggested a latent capacity to leap, a latent astonishing celerity and strength, that could crush at one blow. Yet his speech was simple and suave, perfectly decided and strangely frank. He had some thoughts, he said, of becoming a clergyman. He seemed observant, meditative, as if comparing whatever he saw with something in his mind's eye. As he looked out of the window at the muddy paths and shabby grass, the elms standing scattered at equal intervals, the ugly factory-like buildings, and the loud-voiced youths passing by, dressed like shop-assistants, I

---

[1] Herbert Lyman.

44

could well conceive his thoughts, and I said apologetically that after Oxford all this must seem to him rather mean; and he replied curtly: "Yes, it does." I explained our manner of life, our social distinctions, our choice of studies, our sports, our food, our town amusements. He listened politely, obviously rather entertained and not displeased to find that, according to my description, all I described might be dismissed forever without further thought. Then he sat good-naturedly on the floor and began to look at my books—a rather meagre collection in some open shelves. He spied Swinburne's *Poems,* and took out the volume. Did I like Swinburne? Yes, perhaps he was rather verbose; but did I know the choruses in *Atalanta in Calydon?* No? Then he would read me one. And he read them all, rather liturgically, with a perfect precision and clearness, intoning them almost, in a sort of rhythmic chant, and letting the strong meaning shine through the steady processional march of the words. It seemed the more inspired and oracular for not being brought out by any human change of tone or of emphasis. I had not heard poetry read in this way before. I had not known that the English language could become, like stained glass, an object and a delight in itself.

He stayed a long time, until, the daylight having decidedly failed, he remembered that he was to dine at the Jameses'. My own dinner was long since cold. He was off the next day, he said; but I must look him up whenever I came to London. I saw no more of him at that time; but I received through the post a thin little book bound in white vellum, *The Bookbills of Narcissus,* by Richard Le Gallienne, inscribed "from R." And William James not long afterwards took occasion to interrupt himself, as his manner was, as if a sudden thought had struck him, and to say to me: "I hear you have seen this young grandson of Lord John Russell's. He talked about you; you seem to have made an impression." The impression I had made was that I was capable of receiving impressions. With young Russell, who completely ignored society and convention, this was the royal road to friendship.

When late in March of the following year, 1887, after the

winter semester at Berlin, I reached England for the holidays,
Russell was not in town, but wrote that he was bringing a boat
down from the engineers at Newbury to the boatbuilders in
London. They were merely patched up for the journey; it would
be a three days' trip, one on a canal and two on the Thames. He
feared he couldn't offer me much accommodation and I should
have to sleep ashore, but it would be a good chance of seeing the
river. It was finally arranged that I should join him on the second
day at Reading. Muddy and sordid streets led from the dismal
railway station to the Kennet Canal Office where Russell's small
yacht, the *Royal,* was to lie for the night. After various inquiries
I found my way over a shaky plank (very little to my taste) to a
narrow strip of deck surrounding the cabin skylight. There I
found my host in conversation with a workman. My arrival was
noticed, and I was asked if I had duly deposited my bag at the
inn. All being well, I was left to stand about, while the conversation with the workman continued. I stood by for a while and
listened; but seeing that the business gave no signs of coming to
an end, and was not very intelligible or interesting, I sat on the
edge of the cockpit and took to sketching the hulks, masts and
chimneys visible from the river. In those days I always carried a
note-book and pencil in my pocket for setting down sudden inspirations. I had full time for exhausting the dreary beauties of the
scene and my small skill in expressing them. At length the worthy
workman departed (I suppose his working hours were up) and
Russell called me, quite affectionately, slipped his arm into mine,
and took me to look at the cabin and the engine-room and the
galley, which was also the place where one washed. My ignorant
questions were answered briefly, clearly, with instant discernment
of what I knew and didn't know about ships. Then we went
ashore for tea.

Russell said he should not have been a peer but an engineer.
At the time I thought this a little joke, remembering him reading
the choruses in *Atalanta* and wishing to be a parson; but now I
see that there was a genuine feeling in it. When he died, one of

the notices in the newspapers referred to his "scientific training" and its value in his political career. What was this scientific training? Surely nothing that he acquired at Winchester or Oxford, but what he learned while refitting his steam-yacht and talking to workmen, as he had that afternoon. He took up each mechanical novelty as it arose, experimented, became more or less expert. He carved, drove and steered admirably; he would have made an excellent naval officer and gunner. When he lived at Broom Hall and had a private electric plant for charging his launch and supplying his light, I remember asking him what electricity was. And he said, "I will show you," and after making me leave my watch at a distance, he brought me close to the large magnet that formed part of the machinery, until I felt a strong pull; and then he said triumphantly, "That is what it is." In one sense, a scholastic and verbal answer; yet there was the scientific humility and peace in it that is satisfied with dark facts. And there was another side to his pleasure in engineering: the sense of mastery. Matter can be wooed, coaxed, and mastered like a woman, and this without being in the least understood sympathetically. On the contrary the keen edge of the pleasure comes from defiance. If matter can crush us when ignored, it can be played with and dragged about when once caught in its own meshes: and this skillful exercise of compulsion was dear to Russell. When he acted as Leader of the Opposition in the House of Lords he was not half so happy or in his element. The peers could not so easily be engineered.

At the inn he began to lavish endearments on the cat, who returned his advances disdainfully, and after purring a little when stroked found the thing a bore and scooted into parts unknown. The barmaid then had her turn for a moment, and would doubtless have proved more responsive; but the other servants had to be spoken to about the tea—the tea was very important—and the smiling barmaid and the ungrateful cat were alike forgotten. Tea was a wonderful sedative; and the post and the newspapers were brought in at the same time. Russell opened his letters with the tips of his strong fingers, without haste, without one needless movement or the least unnecessary force. A brief glance usually sufficed, and the letter was dropped, as if into eternal oblivion, upon the floor. But now and then something called for a comment, and then my presence seemed providential. I was invited to observe the stupidity of the correspondent or the folly of the government, or the outrage it was to have such prolonged bad weather. What did I think of the absurd language of the Scottish housekeeper who asked: "Will I light the fire?" And could I conceive anything more annoying than the position of a young man who hadn't yet come into his money and whose grandmother (Lady Russell, and not Lady Stanley) was a fool? In all this fault-finding there was nothing really troubled or querulous. It was all serene observation of the perversity of things, the just perceptions and judgments of a young god to whom wrongness was hateful on principle, but who was not in the least disturbed about it in his own person. Was it not his own choice to move in this ridiculous world, where there were imperfect inns and yachts to be refitted and untrustworthy tradesmen and faithless cats and silly, disappointed barmaids? What difference could such incidents of travel make to a transcendental spirit, fixed and inviolate in its own centre?

The next day early we started down the river in the *Royal*. She was a steam yacht of 100 tons, rigged at sea, I was told, as a schooner, but now mastless. There was a cockpit aft, with a seat round it, and the wheel in the middle; my ecclesiastical mind at once compared it to the apse of a primitive basilica, with its semicircle of stalls and its bishop's throne in the centre, whence the pilot of souls might rise and lay his hands on the altar; in this case, the wheel. Two or three steep steps led below, from this cockpit, into the cabin, which occupied the whole width of the boat and perhaps a third of her length. There were some lockers on either side, and two broad bunks beyond, supplied with red plush mattresses and pillows. The table between had flaps that could be let down, leaving only a ledge some six inches wide running down its length; two other sleeping places could then be arranged on the floor between the table and the bunks; but we were never more than two when I was on board. The cabin was sealed at the end by a varnished yellow bulkhead, decorated with a large barometer and a small clock. To go forward it was necessary to skirt the cabin roof, with its row of square lights, along the edge of the deck. There was a cabin boy who cooked and served our meals quite properly and might well have been called a steward. The two or three other men of the crew I hardly ever saw during the three weeks I spent, the following year, on board the *Royal*.

At such close quarters I soon began to understand what was expected of me. I was liked, I was wanted, I was confided in, but only when my turn came, when other interests flagged and nothing urgent was to be done. I should not have been liked, or wanted, or confided in if I had interfered with other things or made myself a nuisance. But as a sympathetic figure in the background, to whom Olympian comments were always intelligible, I fitted in very well. Being an unpractical person, a foreigner, and a guest, I naturally accepted everything as it came; and being indolent but meditative, with eyes for the new scenes before me, I was never better entertained than when neglected, or busier than when idle. Moreover, I was left free and had my escapades. In later years Russell, who was no pedestrian, liked to plan my walks for me and did it very well. His topographical sense was excellent, and in driving or motoring about he noticed and remembered every nook and every prospect. When asked for directions he liked to give them; it was a pleasure to his executive mind. So the next morning, when we arrived at Windsor and were stopping for some supplies, I was allowed half an hour ashore, and advised to go up to the Castle terrace: but I mustn't loiter, for in all Russell's mighty movements punctuality was absolutely demanded.

In the lovely misty sunshine of that April morning, I climbed the outer Castle steps, not without profound emotion. I was treading the steps of Windsor Castle. The Thames valley stretched

before me, green and rural, peopled and living. Eton lay at my
feet: I could distinguish the great east window of the Chapel,
and the wooden turrets. The fields, the trees, the river glittered
mildly in the sun, as if all atremble with dew. What homeliness,
what simplicity in this grandeur! How modest were these important places, how silent, how humbly faithful to the human scale!
If such gentle discipline could conquer the world, why should it
not conquer the heart? But I mustn't sentimentalise too long, or
my rebellious friend below—horrible thought!—might be kept waiting. Strange that being the heir to so many privileges he should
appreciate them so little, and should use the strength that he derived from tradition in deriding tradition and in destroying it.

My position as a familiar friend who was not a nuisance was
not established without some preliminary slips. One was a slip in
the literal sense of the word. Russell had at Hampton, where he
then lived, an electric launch for scurrying at a surprising speed
along the river. Electric launches were novelties in those days, and
with his good steering and perfect serenity, he attracted the admiring attention of the good people in the boats or on the banks.
But nature had endowed him with a more surprising ability of
another kind. He could walk along the edges and ledges of roofs,
and up inclined poles, like a cat. I suppose all boys, except me,
have had a desire to do such things, and have tried their hand
at them at a certain age, and then abandoned feline ambitions
for things more human. But in Russell, for some reason, feline
instincts survived, and developed into habits. He performed his
acrobatic feats as a matter of course, without training and without
comment. He never boasted of them; he only thought it a singular
deficiency in others not to be able to do them. One Sunday afternoon we had landed at Richmond for tea, and on our return
found the launch removed from the landing—there was naturally
a crowd of trippers on that day—and it lay at a little distance
from the sloping bank, which didn't allow it to come nearer. For
Russell this created no problem. One long boathook was turned
into a bridge from the launch to the shore, and seizing the other

as a *picador* does his lance, and sticking the prong through the clear water into the sand, he walked calmly and quickly aboard. But how was I to get in? In the same way of course. In vain did I protest, like Rosencrantz and Guildenstern, that I hadn't the skill. Hamlet said it was as easy as lying. If I had insisted on making them turn about, and wait for their chance to come up to the landing so that I might step aboard easily, I should have been making myself a nuisance. Seeing my hesitation, Russell said encouragingly: "Come on. Try it. I'll lend you a hand." I knew I should fall in; but I might as well try it, since the only alternative was to wade across, and I must get wet in any case. The pole was rather steep, I had on ordinary boots, not tennis shoes like Russell, and no experience in walking the tight rope. So I took the boathook and gave Russell my other hand. The result was tragic, but not what either of us expected. I fell in, inevitably, but I pulled him in after me; and while I only got my legs wet, he fell in backwards head over heels, with a tremendous splash, which caused great laughter among the sundry trippers lined up on the shore. There was no danger, even in a complete immersion; two feet of water at most, and a warm summer afternoon. We both climbed in easily; but Russell flew into an indescribable rage. His language showed that the society of workingmen had not been wasted upon him; or rather that he must have overheard a good deal that no workingman would knowingly have said in his presence. Where? Or could nature have endowed him with Billingsgate as it had endowed him with somnambulism when awake? For that inexhaustible flow of foul words and blasphemous curses was somnambulistic: he didn't know what he was saying or why. It was an automatism let loose, as was his acrobatic instinct.

I thought at the time that what maddened him was having been baulked and made a fool of in public; but now that I know him better I believe that he had no idea that he was in the least to blame. He felt innocent and injured. It was all my fault for being such an incredible muff. I had ducked him in the Thames and was keeping him wet to the skin in the cool breeze all the way home. His memory for injuries, however—and he thought everybody injured him—was remarkably short. As soon as he got into dry clothes his wrath subsided. Still, he had been so outrageously abusive, and so persistent, that I was cut to the quick. Not that I minded his words, which I had hardly distinguished and couldn't remember; they had no real application to me and couldn't stick. What I feared was that the sting of his own folly had made him hate me, and that all might be over between us. But not in the least. He didn't understand why that evening I could hardly swallow my food, or why I was leaving the next morning.

There was some difficulty about getting my things to the station. It wasn't far, and I had only a bag, but it was rather heavy. "I'll carry it for you," he said; and he actually did so, most of the way. And he continued to send me little notes, inviting me to this or that so long as I remained in England; and before long, instead of signing them "yours sincerely," he began to sign them "yours ever." This was not meant for a mute apology, kindness vanquishing resentment. He behaved exactly in the same way with his worst enemies, such as Lady Scott: forgot terrible injuries, and reverted spontaneously to a deeper impulse, which events had obscured for a moment. I accepted all his invitations. My ego was no less absolute than his, and calmer. If he allowed me my inabilities, I could allow him his explosions. That the wild animal and the furious will should exist beneath his outwardly exact and critical intelligence was so much added, a double *virtù*. I liked it and I didn't fear it.

The astonishing thing about this incident was that Russell completely forgot it. Years after, when I once referred to having pulled him into the water at Richmond, he denied it, and didn't know what I was talking about. This again was not a case of legal oblivion, such as lawyers command a man to scatter over his past when he is about to give evidence: it was a genuine blank. A blank, that is, in his conscious memory; for in his inner man the thing must have left its trace, because he never afterwards urged me to do anything to which I was not inclined or taxed me with any defect. He respected my freedom unconditionally and gladly, as I respected his. This was one of the reasons why our friendship lasted so many years, weathering all changes in our circumstances, in spite of the few points of contact between our characters and the utter diversity in our lives. Neither of us was ever a nuisance to the other.

When I was about to make my first visit to Oxford, I had received four notes of introduction, enclosed in the following letter:

Ferishtah, Hampton
21 Ap. 1887.

Dear Santayana,

I find that the number of my intimate friends actually at Oxford is much decreased. Natheless I send you 4 to: 1 Burke of Trinity, 2 Jepson of Balliol, 3 Johnson of New, 4 Davis of Balliol.

1 is a friend of 8 or 10 years standing, a good fellow but so terrible reserved that you'll get nothing out of him.

2 is a funny fellow of immoral tendencies and pessimistic affectation. Well worth your visit to make him show off.

3 is the man I most admire and—in the world, knows every book that is, transcendentalist, genius, and is called affected. The way for you to treat him is to take no notice when he tries (as he will) to shock you. If he discourses, listen: it will be worth while.

4 is a strictly moral Radical Positivist. You may label him with all the 'ists suitable to that combination. He will only talk politics to you but has more heart than he shows on the surface. Still of course he's a Philistine.

Eh voilà!

Yours sincerely,
RUSSELL.

Write to me in about a week.

Number One in this list was not number one by accident. Perhaps I got nothing out of him, but I liked him very much. He was sensitive and brave. You felt that in some way he must have suffered a great deal. Had it been bad health, family quarrels, love, or perhaps some disgrace? He was Irish, but Protestant, very Protestant in a profound, silent, unhappy way. Intense moral feeling, intense sense of the difference between the better and the worse. He had been with Russell at a private school, and had a good education, but felt very Irish, and perhaps regretted that his money came from a brewery—*Burke's Ales, Stout and Porter*. We talked chiefly about Russell, whom he cared for; but caring didn't modify his strict standards, and while he could forgive Russell's commonplace peccadilloes, when it came later to his treatment of the Billings girls, whom Burke knew, he became intractable, and broke with him. As I wasn't going to desert Russell for that, or for anything, Burke and I ceased to keep up our acquaintance.

I found Number Two in comfortable not very academic lodgings, the best available no doubt, yet hardly worthy of his ornamental person. He was not really good-looking, but his hair was yellow, parted in the middle and carefully waved, like a ploughed field. He said his life was devoted to the culture of it. Incidentally, however, he had accomplished a greater thing. He had already, at twenty, doubled human knowledge in one of the sciences, the science *de modis veneris*. There had been forty modes before, now there were eighty. He didn't show me the classic designs for those forty modes; they are probably not extant; nor did he reveal the secret of his new variations. I was sceptical, and Jepson didn't interest me.

Number Three was then in his first year at New College. He had rooms at the top of the new buildings overlooking Holywell. Over the roofs of the low houses opposite, the trees in the Parks were visible in places, as well as the country beyond: and pointing to the distant horizon Lionel Johnson said sadly: "Everything above that line is right, everything below it is wrong." These were almost the first words he spoke to me, and they formed an admirable preface to a religious conversion.

He was rather a little fellow, pale, with small sunken blinking eyes, a sensitive mouth, and lank pale brown hair. His child-like figure was crowned by a smooth head, like a large egg standing on its small end. His age was said to be sixteen, and I readily believed the report. His genius was the kind that may be precocious, being an inward protest against external evidence; and his aspect, though thoughtful, was very youthful: yet his real age seems to have been twenty, only a year and a half younger than Russell and three years younger than I. He said he lived on eggs in the morning and nothing but tea and cigarettes during the rest of the day. He seldom went out, but when he did, it was for a walk of twenty miles in the country: and on those days he dined. There was also conspicuous on a centre table a jug of Glengarry whiskey between two open books: *Les Fleurs du Mal* and *Leaves of Grass*. Two large portraits hung on the wall: Cardinal Newman and Cardinal Wiseman. When he was of age he intended to become a Catholic and a monk: at present his people, who were Welsh, objected. This intention he carried out in part; but instead of becoming a monk he became a Fenian; for at the same time that he was converted from a legal Protestant to a legal Catholic, he was mystically transformed from a Welshman into an Irishman. It was the same thing, he said, being Celtic. Perhaps, too, being Irish was closer to his inner man, and certainly more congruous with Catholicism and with whiskey.

Our acquaintance was never close, but it seemed to gain in interest, for both of us, as it receded. Some years later he honoured me with a poem *To a Spanish Friend,* beginning with the words "Exiled in America," and ending with an exhortation to return to Saint Theresa and her "holy Avila." I returned often, and should gladly have grown old in that atmosphere, yet not in order to indulge the impulse to dream awake: rather in order to remove the pressure of reality (of which I was only too well aware) and to leave my reflexion free to survey that reality fairly, at arm's length. Lionel Johnson lived only in his upper storey, in a loggia open to the sky; and he forgot that he had climbed there up a long flight of flinty steps, and that his *campanile* rested on the vulgar earth. The absence of all foundations, of all concreteness, of all distinction between fiction and truth, makes his poetry indigestible. I see that it is genuine poetry—an irresponsible flux of impassioned words: and his religion too was genuine religion, if we admit that religion must be essentially histrionic. Let everything that comes, it says, be to thee an Angel of the Lord; embroider upon it in that sense, and let the vulgar world recede into a distant background for an endless flapping of angelic wings and chanting of angelic voices. The age had given Lionel Johnson enough verbal culture and knowledge of literature to raise his effusions in that angelic choir to a certain level of refinement and fancy; but he was not a traditional Catholic, accepting good-naturedly a supernatural economy that happened to prevail in the universe, as political and domestic economy prevail in one's earthly fortunes. Nor was he a philosopher, enduring the truth. He was a spiritual rebel, a spiritual waif who couldn't endure the truth, but demanded a lovelier fiction to revel in, invented or accepted it, and called it revelation. In part like Shelley, in part like Rimbaud, he despised the world and adored the unreal.

Had that first saying of his to me, that everything above the horizon was right and everything below it wrong, represented his primary and constant mind, he might have become a monk as he had intended; because that is the foundation of Christianity. There is a divine world *surrounding us;* but there is sin and damnation *in us.* Lionel Johnson never seemed to me to feel this as, for instance, St. Paul and St. Augustine felt it. What he felt was rather the opposite, that everything within him was right, and everything outside wrong; and if he made an exception of the blank sky, this was only because he could fill it at will with his poetry. In other words, he was a transcendentalist and a humanist; for that reason he seemed a prophet to Russell; and at bottom nothing could be more contrary to Christian humility and to Catholic discipline. I know that an effort has been made to represent him as a saint, hushing the sad reality: it is part of the general practice of bluff, silence, and the *claque* in journalistic criticism. Let me give some grounds for a contrary opinion.

Russell, who was faithful to the inspired friend of his school days and completely ignored his conversion and Catholicism, published a collection of Johnson's letters from Winchester, written when he was seventeen or eighteen years old. Here are some extracts: "I do not love sensuality: I do not hate it: I do not love purity: I do not hate it; I regard both as artistic aspects of life."

"A man's life is not his acts of profession: drills, sermons, deathbeds, stone-breaking are not life: the life is the sunsets we worship, the books we read, the faces we love."

"I tell you, be happy, for that is to know God; be sinful, for that is to feel God; be all things, for that is to be God."

"At my worst moments I see myself Archbishop and Poet Laureate, at my best I don't see myself at all, but merely God and other men and the world and my dear art."

"I think that my earlier scriptures were the spiritualised expression of my life-long faith—I adopted the language of convenient morality to apply it to the immoral doctrines of my personal gospel."

After two years of Oxford, Johnson had developed an element of banter, and favoured me with the following letter:

Hunter's Inn,
August 2nd (1888)   Hedder's Mouth, Barnstable.
My dear Santayana,

Forgive my not writing earlier: I have been for weeks a wanderer, with letters chasing me about the world in vain.

I wish I could be in Oxford in August; but only, be sure, for the sake of meeting you. Unhappily it is impossible. I am bound, hand and foot, to a "reading party" in an obscure corner of Devonshire; and see no prospect of escape. Can you not find your way to our pastoral retreat? or be in Oxford in October? You will not go back to our dear America just yet, mon ami?

Berenson charmed Oxford for a term, and vanished: leaving behind a memory of exotic epigrams and, so to speak, cynical music. It was a strangely curious time. He is something too misanthropic: but always adorable.

I missed Russell lately by four hours: you know we have not met for many a year, almost. I incline to think it time for his drama of life to become critical in some way: at least, beyond disregarding all unities of time and space he does not appear to progress. This morning is very hot; the sea sparkles; Plato is beautiful; the world very charming; but why go to America? Come to Oxford in October and learn of me how to live on nothing with nothing to do. I intend to teach Berenson: and neither of you shall set foot again in Boston, that Holy and self-satisfied city.

Do you read Shelley still, and have you renounced that stage devil, Byron, and all his works, except Don Juan? Kegan Paul, whom you met, asked me the question concerning you the other day. Ach! there is always Keats.

When next you hear from me you will probably hear that I am a Jesuit novice or a budding Carthusian or some such an one. Anyway, the Church will probably have claimed her own in me. But just now I am lazy and fond of life this side of death.

Will you let me know your movements? And pray think out ways and means to see us all before you go to the Land of the Lost, and leave us desolate!

Yours very sincerely,

Lionel Johnson.

This was written at the moment when the vogue of aestheticism, pessimism, preraphaelitism, and amateur Catholicism was at its height. The superior young mind was bound to share these affectations, but might save itself by a mental reservation and a pervasively weary, all-knowing and all-mocking tone. Was Lionel

Johnson laughing at Jesuits and Carthusians, at Plato, Shelley
and Keats, no less than at Berenson and me? Or had something
or somebody, Shelley perhaps or the Jesuits, really taken him in?
I have no doubt that sincerity existed somewhere beneath all these
poses, but the exact place of it is hard to discover. Russell at that
moment, in the drama of his life, was making rapid progress in
the direction of Byron's *Don Juan*: he had fallen into the clutches
of a mature adventuress who was marrying him off to her daughter. In what direction was Lionel Johnson's sincere drama pro-
gressing?

I am not writing Johnson's life or Russell's or even my own,
but only picking out such points as interest me now in my personal retrospect. I saw Lionel Johnson in later years only at long
intervals and found him each time less accessible. My last glimpse
of him was in the summer of 1897, in Russell's rooms in Temple
Gardens. It was a tragic spectacle. He still looked very young,
though he was thirty, but pale, haggard, and trembling. He stood
by the fireplace, with a tall glass of whiskey and soda at his elbow,
and talked wildly of persecution. The police, he said, were after
him everywhere. Detectives who pretended to be friends of his
friend Murphy or of his friend MacLaughlin had to be defied.
Without a signed letter of introduction he could trust nobody.
He had perpetually to sport his oak. As he spoke, he quivered
with excitement, hatred, and imagined terrors. He seemed to be
living in a dream; and when at last he found his glass empty, it
was with uncertainty that his hat sat on his head as with sudden
determination he made for the door, and left us without saying
good night.

I never saw him again, but he still lived for five years, and
there may have been important changes in him before the end.
Nor do I profess to have fathomed his Celtic inspiration or his
Celtic Catholicism. He says in his lines on *Wales*:

> *No alien hearts may know that magic, which acquaints*
> *Thy heart with splendid passion, a great fire of dreams;*

and I am willing to believe him. But to my prosaic apprehension he remains a child of premature genius and perpetual immaturity; and I cannot forget what Oscar Wilde is reported to have said of him, that any morning at eleven o'clock you might see him come out very drunk from the Café Royal, and hail the first passing perambulator. Yet I should be the last to deride the haze in which he lived, on the ground that Bacchus had something to do with it. Bacchus too was a god; and the material occasion of inspiration makes no difference if the spirit is thereby really liberated. Lionel Johnson lived in the spirit; but to my sense his spirituality was that of a transcendental poet, not that of a saint. His mind was subjective in its presuppositions or in the absence of all presuppositions; so that after reading him through you are aware of a great wind of passionate language, but not of what was said or of what it all was about. And this vagueness was hardly due to absorption in something higher, because it did not liberate him from everything lower. So at least he tells us in *The Dark Angel*.

> *Because of thee, no thought, no thing*
> *Abides for me undesecrate . . .*
> *Of two defeats, of two despairs;*
> *Less dread, a change to drifting dust,*
> *Than thine eternity of cares.*

And if we ask what the alternative to these two despairs may be, and what will issue from the triumph that he still hopes for, we find nothing positive, nothing specific, but only transcendental spirit, still open to every thought and to every torment:

> *Lonely, unto the Lone I go;*
> *Divine, to the Divinity.*

These words are the words of Plotinus and of Christian mystics; but here we do not feel them to be backed by either the Platonic or the Christian scheme of the universe: they are floating words. Even the firmness and constructive power of the Catholic faith could not *naturalise* Lionel Johnson in the Catholic world. The same emotional absolutism, the same hatred of everything not plastic to the fancy, which drove him from Victorian England into Celtic poetry and Catholic supernaturalism, kept him from accepting definition and limitation even there; he could not deny himself other dreams. As he writes in *Gwynedd*:

> *We will not wander from this land;* [Wales]
> *Here distress*
> *Dreams, and delight dreams: dreaming, we can fill*
> *All solitary haunts with prophecy,*
> *All heights with holiness and mystery;*
> *Our hearts with understanding, and our will*
> *With love of nature's law and loveliness.*

The last two lines may seem to contradict what I am saying, but I quote them in order to be fair. Understanding, with love of nature's law, if it were real understanding of the true law of nature, would stop all that dreaming, or reduce it to wasted time and gratuitous trouble, as he himself says in *The Dark Angel*, already quoted:

> *Because of thee, the land of dreams*
> *Becomes a gathering-place of fears:*
> *Until tormented slumber seems*
> *One vehemence of useless tears.*

But the word nature, in a Celtic poet, does not mean what it meant to Lucretius, nor understanding what it meant to Aristotle, nor law what it meant to Newton. These words mean rather landscape, divination, and magic; as, in the line about Wales, where he says he will not leave *this land,* he means the *soul* of this land, which is the land of dreams.

The passionate need of sinking into these dreams, and defying the false world that pretended to be more real, seems to me to have been the secret of Lionel Johnson in all his phases. It was

what made him a pagan or a Buddhist at Winchester, a Baude-
lairean Catholic at Oxford, and a Fenian conspirator in London.
In his verse he could modulate those dreams lyrically, but not
logically, morally, and historically as the Church had modulated
her original inspirations; and he dared to take them, as the Church
did hers, for revelations of the truth. But his dreams had no such
application to the facts and sorrows of life as had the Christian
faith. Their passion remained dreamy, weak and verbal, and he
perished not a martyr to his inspiration, but a victim of it.

Now to return to Russell. In their adolescence both he and
Lionel Johnson had revelled in transcendental liberty: but Russell
was strong, and exposed to the dangers and vices of strength, as
Johnson to those of weakness. Russell had no gift of fancy: he
had to be satisfied with the vulgar plots that real life furnishes
willy-nilly to the spirit; and he sank into them desperately, without discrimination and without taste. Yet his strong intelligence,
rather conventional in worldly matters, remained conscious that
it was being deceived. This early transcendentalism was not apparent in him; his wives, I expect, never understood that it was
there; yet I think it helped to make him reckless in choosing and
in divorcing them. For him it was all a desperate and worthless
gamble in any case. Any lust, any convenience, any enterprise,
any stale moral or political nostrum would do to play with: the
point was to dream your dream out, and to have your way in it.

This is my interpretation: but in a letter written a fortnight
before his death—almost the last I received from him—he puts the
matter in the following words:

"It is not really the case that Lionel lies in the limbo of almost
incredible things. On the contrary, all that is the real part of me
and my very extensive external activities are to me of the nature
of Maya or illusion. They interest me, they are my job, and I do
them, but they are not part of my real life. I am surprised that
you should say that I minimise my friendship of Lionel, to all
intimate friends I have always admitted that he was my dearest
friend and the greatest influence in my life, but I seldom take

the public into my confidence about my real feelings. I received two great shocks in my life; the first being when Jowett sent me down— My rage and mortification at being so wronged produced a bitterness and permanently injured my character. Finally, when Elizabeth left me I went completely dead and have never come alive again. She never realised how I worshipped and loved her, and how I idealised what is in essence a worthless character, and her light-hearted cruelty killed something in me which has never revived. Since 1918 I have had neither ambition, nor enthusiasm, nor interest nor will to live, and I ascribe my bad heart entirely to the year's anguish I suffered after she left me and her betrayal with a kiss of Judas. Still, as you say I obliterate my feelings so easily, no doubt you will not believe this."

No: I didn't believe *all* this; the words about Elisabeth didn't ring true in my ears. But I believed and believe what he says about Lionel Johnson, which is what concerns me here; and I can also credit his living "dead," precisely when he was a member of the Government, busy and rehabilitated officially and financially. It would have been an experience such as in my own case I call somnambulistic, under which I may be doing mechanically what some people think my best work. He had transcendental insight, acquired in his adolescence (the natural time for it) under the influence of Lionel Johnson: and this common spiritual challenge to the dream of life raised their friendship to a great height and made it constant in spite of all obstacles and external disparities. Neither Johnson's Catholicism and drink, nor Russell's matrimonial imbroglios did justice to their inner man; such commitments were accidents, as was their vulgar politics also; and both knew it. I also divined it in them, but from the outside, and I am glad to have this confession of Russell's, written almost on his deathbed, to buttress my divination. Transcendental rebellion, like that of Lucifer, lay at the bottom of his heart, but buried like a prehistoric civilisation under layer upon layer of ruins. Lionel Johnson could display this spirit lyrically and publish it to the puzzled world in his talk and in his poems; but poor Russell had only his ruins to display and to be judged by most unjustly, ruins of passions that had hounded him through life like a succession of nightmares, and had made the gossips call him "The Wicked Earl."

But let me return to the pleasant summer of 1887, when under his auspices I first felt the full charm of England. His last invitation before I left for Spain took me to Winchester. He was staying at his old Housemaster's for the School celebration of the Queen's Jubilee, and he took a room for me at an inn. In this way I had the advantage of being guided, introduced, and shown what there was to see, and also the advantage of being left alone so as to see it. This was my first acquaintance with an English public school. Externally the flint walls and low buildings prepared me for mediaeval austerity; but at the Commemoration service in the chapel it was the soul of modern England that stirred under those Gothic arches and windows, and knelt or sang in those monastic stalls. Deeply moving was the singing by the whole School in unison of *God Save the Queen*, all the verses, under the spell of restrained emotion: fifty years of safety and glory behind, and before, for those young spirits, the promise and the uncertainties of a broad future. This was more than ten years before the Boer War, before the first hint of difficulty and limitation in British dominion. Nothing as yet impaired the sense of a glorious heritage committed to the care of the rising generation, to be maintained and enriched indefinitely. The pride of earth merged delusively and overpoweringly with the will of heaven.

We lunched with one of the masters, Mr. Richardson, whose amiable wife seemed to have a mother's heart for all the boys, and among them for Russell. She perceived that I cared for him and instantly became friendly and confidential. Winchester was the only place where he was loved. Ten years later, when I went with him there again for a hearing connected with the trial of Lady Scott, Mrs. Dick, as she was called, said to me: "We would all perjure ourselves for him." The act was hardly necessary, but the readiness showed the right spirit. Justice is before the law, moral reality above moral shams; and in that trial everything was a sham, and yet substantial justice was done in the end. It is the English way.

In the evening I went again to the chapel. This time I was alone, and from my corner I drank in the memorable spectacle, more memorable for being something usual and the crown of every school day. The boys were less restless at that hour; fatigue and darkness cut off distractions; the spirit of the place, the language of the prayers, had a chance of attuning the senses to their ancient music. That everything external was perfunctory rather helped something internal to become dominant. I saw some boys bury their faces in their folded arms, not (it seemed to me) affectedly, but as if seeking solitude, as if fleeing to the wilderness, carried by a wave of juvenile devotion. How well I knew that plight! Adolescence, in its pregnant vagueness, casts about for some ineffable happiness in the fourth dimension. But how admirable here the setting to give a true pitch to those first notes! This simplicity in wealth protects from vulgarity, these classic poets, when grammar and ferrule are forgotten, leave a sediment of taste and soundness in the mind, and these reticent prayers, with their diplomatic dignity and courtesy, leave it for the heart to say the last word. It is all make-believe, as sports are: but in both those dramatic exercises there is excellent discipline, and the art of life is half learned when they have been practiced and outgrown. What has been learned is the right manner, the just sentiments. It remains to discover the real occasions and the real risks.

In Avila, late in September, I had word from Russell, at Toulouse, "the little 'Royal' is now not far from the Pyrenees . . . We shall be at Marseilles in a week or 10 days and stay there a fortnight. I should be only too pleased if you would join us there en route for Naples." His notions of travel and of foreign parts were those of the British naval man that he ought to have been. To go to Spain you took ship to Lisbon, and to get out you took ship at Barcelona for Marseilles. He was bringing the *Royal* over the *Canal du Midi* from Bordeaux to Narbonne, and back over the *Canal de Bourgogne* from Marseilles to Havre. The yacht was too small for the high seas, and her draught just not too great for those inland shallows. Naples and Sicily had been familiar to him in his childhood: he had spent long seasons there with his parents: but intervening places had little hold on his imagination. My way of travelling from one cathedral town to another he called "getting lost among the railways." Naturally, joining the *Royal* in the Mediterranean was impossible for me, living as I did on a Harvard Fellowship for study in Germany. But his lordship took another view of the matter. "What you say about reading sounds nonsense," he wrote in October. "I should say a 'travelling fellowship' meant *travel* and keep your eyes open, not settle down in a hole to mug." But before the end of November his own spirits had flagged. He was at Civitavecchia, and wrote: "We have had vile weather—rain, cold and lots of wind and sea: and tho' the little boat has behaved wonderfully, you would scarcely have appreciated it . . . Thynne left me at Savona, Roberts never came, Jepson leaves me here . . . I shall probably lay up the 'Royal' at Naples, and come home about the New Year." In May, however, he was back in Italy, coasting from port to port after the fashion of the ancients. "I wish you would join me at Marseilles for the canal journey thro' France," he wrote, "as I shall be quite alone, and it will be a trip than wh. there could not be [anything] more pleasant or more lotus eating."

By that time I had given up all hope of profiting by a longer stay in Germany and had decided to return to Harvard to complete my studies for the doctorate. I would spend my last summer at Avila; but on the way, why shouldn't I join Russell, not at Marseilles but somewhere on the Rhône, and go with him as far as Paris? This was arranged, and I met him at Valence, early in June.

It was an inland voyage of three weeks up and down innumerable locks, through a country wilder and more deserted than I should have thought existed in France. The rivers, whether flow-

ing southward or northward, were wider and swifter than they
seem when looked at from the banks, and seen as pictures, not felt
as powers. The banks, too, for the most part, without being moun-
tainous, looked strangely primitive and unkempt. Such they must
have been when Cæsar and his Gaulish chieftains took them for
boundaries, or forded them with warlike cries. In sympathy with
those rude predecessors (or because my razors were dull and toilet
on board difficult to manage) I let my beard grow: an experiment
that I repeated twenty years later, much in the same spirit and
ultimately with the same negative result. Being primitive and
"natural" does very well when it is inevitable and unconscious;
but it is a mistake and a perverse affectation when it is intentional.
I shaved again that summer as soon as I got to Paris and to a
decent barber; and I shaved again in 1912 when I left Harvard
and began life afresh as an elderly gentleman of leisure.

Russell spoke French readily and not incorrectly, with a strong
English accent, and when speaking it he put on an air of genial
assurance (rather American, I thought) entirely absent from the
quiet precision of his usual conversation; and he did the same
when he spoke in England in public. It was the second thickness
of the veil of Maya wrapping and smothering his transcendental
self. The first layer of illusion or shamming plunged him into the
business of this absurd world; the second turned him into a sort
of Low Church Evangelist or middle-class Browningite or unscru-
pulous lawyer, smilingly and victoriously proving the truth of
some palpable lie. He was said to be an excellent debater; but
Lord Curzon was also said to be an eloquent speaker; and when
once I heard him speak in the House of Lords, on an Indian
question which he ought to have known at first hand, he was so
platitudinous and partial in his matter and such a bad actor in
his manner, that I could hardly believe my ears. One of the
French Ministers under Clemenceau, at the end of the war, at a
luncheon given by the de Fontenays, had the same incredibly
vulgar way of repeating party slogans with a false intonation. I
can explain it only by the degradation of taste and intelligence

produced by partisan propaganda. People will shout under the spell of convention things they would shudder to hear in their rational moments.

Two men in their early twenties eating and sleeping for three weeks in the same cabin, seeing the same sights and living through the same incidents without one moment of boredom, without one touch of misunderstanding or displeasure, could not but become very good friends. But we were predestined friends before, in fact ever since our first acquaintance; and I don't think this trip through Burgundy made much difference. Friendship in any case didn't mean for Russell what it meant for me. There was no dramatic curiosity in it for him, no love of speculation and unanimity. He cared nothing about what other people might be in themselves or in their feelings and careers; nor did he have the least need of unbosoming himself. He was frank enough and didn't take pains to disguise facts in his own life, when the interest of the moment led him to refer to them. In that way, during his lawsuits, he told me many secrets by implication; but he never set out to relate his affairs, expressly, for the sake of communication and sympathy. On the contrary, I think he revelled in secrecy. By this time, in France, he already had secrets that he didn't tell me, which I think had not been the case in England the summer before. Thus he said once that he might try his luck at Monte Carlo *again*. I knew nothing of his having been there at all; but I now gathered that he had probably lost a good deal at the tables.

The atmosphere of mystery had become thick, however, when I joined him again in England in August. He had now taken what might be called a mansion, Broom Hall, Teddington, with great old trees and a spacious lawn sloping gently down to the water's edge. The dark red brick house at the top, also spacious without being large, had a quiet old-fashioned air. The place might have seemed a little sad; but Russell was then bent on boating in the Thames and despised fashionable society. For him it seemed to me perfect. It was dignified enough to make a home of, so long as he was a bachelor, where he could have his books and family heirlooms properly placed, and at the same time keep the *Royal* and the electric launch at hand in his private dock. This prospect pleased him, and I found him engrossed in putting in the electric light and other domestic arrangements.

In the afternoon we were to go out in the launch; I was a bit surprised that Jennie, the housemaid, seemed to be coming with us; but I knew she was one of the Billings children. Their mother had been Russell's nurse, and they had played together in their early days. That might be an explanation; but not for the presence of a second young woman, silent and dejected with all her hair loose, already sitting in the stern of the launch, next to the wheel, where Russell would certainly sit. "That is my sister Emma," said Jennie, observing my surprise. I asked if she was drying her hair. No, Lord Russell (Jennie didn't call him "His Lordship") liked her to have it like that. Zo! I said to myself (having been lately in Germany) and I discreetly went to sit with Jennie in the bow, leaving Russell with his dishevelled and rather mad-looking sweetheart in the stern. But how could he be carrying on such an intrigue in public? I thought of Steerforth and Little Emily. And what could be Jennie's position in the matter? An accomplice, a jealous rival, or perhaps a second mistress? For Jennie's eyes were very bright, and she moved about with the freedom of a member of the family, and with some coquetry as well. Accustomed though I was to the wild oats and the love-affairs of my friends, these complications at Broom Hall troubled me a little. It might not prove such a peaceful and dignified retreat as I had fancied. I sailed for America with vague misgivings, and even wrote some verses on Broom Hall that I soon destroyed; yet a phrase or two linger in my memory that seem to have been prophetic. I praised the aspect of the place, then added, *Worse follows better: the wreck of boyish faith and boyish love.*

The next summer I remained in America, preparing my first course of lectures at Harvard. There I received the following letter:

Broom Hall,
Teddington.

23 July 1889.
Dear Santayana,

I am now replying to your letter of May because I have found an answer to your query when the state of lethargy would cease. It has ceased and for the most commonplace of reasons. I have met a young woman and fallen in love with her! and soon I shall be a married man. Could a happier eventuality have occurred? Did I not often say that marriage was my best hope of salvation, only the trouble was to come across anyone I cared about? . . .

Though no doubt the thing is common enough and may be seen every day, still the difference is that the touch of a warm human love has come to *me,* and swamps and sweeps away all cobwebs and ash-heaps in my brain. All my friends and relations say they would not know me. If I ever told you I was satisfied with my situation before, it was a lie and a mere vain attempt to deceive myself.

Write to me and let me know if you will ever be in England or if we must wait till we go to the States to meet you.

Ever yours,
RUSSELL

My appointment at Harvard having been renewed I took a fast steamer in the following June and was in London before the end of the month. There I found the following note awaiting me:

16 June 1890   Walton.
Dear Santayana,

I am so glad to hear you are coming over. I enclose my new address: I am just moving. I shall be so glad to see you and hope you can give me a whole week. . . . Name your own time as I must not miss seeing you. I am so sorry you have only a few days in England. Write me a line as soon as you get this.

Ever yours,
RUSSELL

His new address was Amberley Cottage, Maidenhead. Odd that a newly married man should not mention his wife and still say "I" and not "we"; but Russell was said to resemble Meredith's *Egoist* and perhaps this was a sign of it. When I reached Maidenhead I was met by a little cart with a white pony: here at last was the feminine touch. We drove into a region of newly built villas in small squares of land with young hedges and little trees in curlpapers, and stopped at a flimsy particoloured "cottage," with a shallow tin verandah and the look of never having been lived in. I regretted the lovely lawn and the stately symmetry of Broom Hall: but no doubt the new Lady Russell was "modern," found Teddington impossibly dull and unfashionable, and thought it better to remove Russell from his old associations. Yet why choose this vulgar place? No view, no privacy, no glimpse of the river: a colony of hen-coops in a waste field.

But where was the new Lady Russell? No sign of her in the house, which was almost unfurnished. Even Russell's "office" was bare and carpetless. I saw only a desk, two leather armchairs, and on the mantelpiece a single framed photograph: an oldish but strikingly handsome woman in a ball gown, with great eyes and other conspicuous charms: might have been an emotional actress or a prima donna. It could hardly be Russell's wife: he had spoken of a *young* woman. He noticed that I was examining the photograph attentively and said: "That is Lady Scott."

Lady Scott was his mother-in-law. As I gathered later piecemeal, during the various lawsuits that ensued, she was the daughter of a country parson and had run away to Paris, when still a girl, with a wild young baronet named Sir Claude Scott; they had been married but unhappy, and she had long been a grass widow, with an uncertain income, scouring the borderland between the *monde* and the *demi-monde*. She then lived at Bray and fished in the boating region of the Thames. When she learned that a young and unmarried earl had taken a house not very far from hers, she soon found the means of making his acquaintance. She had a daughter, Mabel Edith, not so handsome as herself but presentable, and brought up like a lapdog amid false luxury and false gaiety. Here was a chance of settling Mabel Edith for life.

If you should read Russell's letter of the previous July, quoted above, without any preconceptions, would you detect anything wrong or queer about it? I think I should have suspected the rhetoric about a warm human love that had made him a new man. But Russell had really undergone a change, "the touch of a warm human love"; only the object of it had not been Mabel Edith. It had been her mother. Or rather, not so much the object of love as the guide to love; for it had been the half-motherly and half-wifely love of a mature woman for a young man physically susceptible but morally crude and insensible. She had overwhelmed him—their letters prove it—in a torrent of effusive sympathy and affection. He had never known a mother's love: "Mrs. Dick's" had come the nearest; but now such a love enveloped him, mixed with all the arts of sensuous seduction and worldly-wise prattle of a woman that had been beautiful and was still appealing. It had been a feast of sincerity, of sympathy, of abounding endearments such as he had never known or dreamt of. Lady Scott persuaded Russell that the way to make him and her friends for life, and guardians of each other's happiness, was for him to marry Mabel Edith. Mabel Edith was insignificant, but she was not less attractive than the housemaids and the lady-secretaries that could so easily seduce him. He would marry her.

Persons of strict morals and limited experience might well cry: Scandalous, monstrous, impossible! What mother would so outrage and deceive her innocent child? Yet in this case the innocent child never complained of her mother: the two remained perfectly united in feeling and policy until death. To pass on Russell to Mabel Edith was, in the eyes of the latter, an act of foresight and love on her mother's part. Wasn't she marrying an important and attractive young man? Didn't she become a Countess? And if the match didn't turn out well, what marriage in the Scotts' social circle had ever turned out well? That would be bad luck, or other people's fault: and Mabel Edith could always sue for divorce, with a tidy alimony. Of course this match couldn't turn out well: and if Lady Scott didn't foresee it, I think her blindness could be due only to the fact that she was in love with Russell herself and in such a welter of emotion and excitement that she was incapable of clear observation or judgment. But poor Mabel Edith—I can't help being sorry for her—very soon discovered the mistake they had made. Russell as a husband, Russell in the domestic sphere, was simply impossible: excessively virtuous and incredibly tyrannical. He didn't allow her enough money or enough liberty. He was punctilious and unforgiving about hours, about truth-telling, about debts. He objected to her friends, her clothes, and borrowed jewels. Moreover, in their intimate relations he was exacting and annoying. She soon hated and feared him. One day she couldn't endure him any longer and ran home to her mother, crying like a frightened child. Her mother clasped her to her bosom, petted her, soothed her; and they began to consider, with their solicitors, how best to get money out of Russell. That loving a man passionately and getting money out of him should go together was no paradox to Lady Scott. It was her ideal of life.

Such were the events, at least as I conceive them, that had caused me to find my friend no longer in the pleasant retreat of Broom Hall, but camping out in an ugly half-furnished villa in a new jerry-built quarter of Maidenhead, without his bride, but with her mother's portrait on the mantelpiece. He was already threatened with two nasty lawsuits: one brought by Emma Billings for breach of promise of marriage, and the other by Mabel Edith for a legal separation on the charge of cruelty.

I had seen enough at Broom Hall to know that in the case of Emma Billings, Russell had something to hide: it was a common seduction, but aggravated by his old relations with the family and by the oddity of some of his demands. Russell was aware of this, and settled the matter out of court; yet a field remained open here where the Scotts might still sow rumours and insinuations. The Oxford scandal was another such field: and both, in a corrupt society, could be used to corroborate the charges of cruelty brought by Mabel Edith. These charges were ridiculous in themselves, except where they touched the intimate relations of the wife and husband: and here they were so embarrassing to describe, and so impossible to prove, that they could serve only to arouse prejudice.

Lady Scott had planned something heroic: to give Russell up as a lover, resign him to her daughter, and keep him only as a dear, dear son and as a source of income. When Mabel Edith spoilt everything by leaving him and declaring war to the knife, her mother's friendly relations with him were not interrupted. "Lady Scott," he wrote to me, "accompanied me to Winchester on a visit to Mrs. Dick and got rather pitched into by her." No wonder; but he seems to have regarded the two matrons as his two godmothers. Lady Scott, in fact, always hoped for a reconciliation, and both mother and daughter kept writing him begging letters. If he proved so heartless as to refuse them all funds, what could they do but threaten? Make peace with us, they said; give us an allowance, or we will ruin your reputation. You are driving us to this against our will, and you know what lovely cues you have given us. Lady Scott felt grievously injured that Russell shouldn't understand her or remember how much she had always loved him.

Thus Russell, at the age of twenty-five, found himself with his back to the wall, and obliged to defend himself in public against scandalous accusations. He was victorious in his two principal trials; but in the meantime he had dilapidated his fortune and forfeited his place in the polite world. This was a greater misfortune than he thought it, because whenever he found himself opposed by a ruling convention he comforted himself with the assertion that he was right and the convention wrong. This self-righteousness only made matters worse; he felt deeply injured, and alienated himself all the more from a world that was less offended than he, and would easily have taken him back. There is nothing sacred about convention: there is nothing sacred about primitive passions or whims; but the fact that a convention exists indicates that a way of living has been devised capable of maintaining itself. I had no more *respect* for the polite world than Russell had, and that was the ground of my sympathy with him: for if convention has the advantage of possessing the field, rebellion against convention has the advantage of springing afresh from the heart, the ultimate judge of everything worth having or doing. Yet a young man with a brilliant career open to him in the world is a fool to flout public opinion, even if he secretly despises it. Peace with the polite world is all-important for one's comfort and euphoria so long as one lives in the polite world.

Luckily Russell's rebellions were not total or radical. They were in fact hereditary, and those of a vast movement long afoot in modern times. He was therefore able to pass into what might be called the anti-polite world, and to play his part there. The Labour Party could take his sermons in gaol at their word, and the verdicts of Courts in his favour as final. They could regard him as morally rehabilitated, and could mend his fortunes by including him in the Government. But Russell was never more desperate than in those last years; British society is sustained by "created interests"; that is to say, by vain commitments into which people have been led unawares, but which it would be too disturbing now to abandon. The farce must be kept up, and it becomes a point of honour to drop dead at last upon the stage, in all one's paint and feathers.

CHAPTER IV

CHANGES IN AVILA

WHEN, after three years, in July, 1886, I returned for the second time to Avila, my arrival had been duly announced by letter for a suitable hour in the afternoon. My father and Don Pelayo were at the station to receive me, and everything at the house was as I had left it. There were no explanations to make. Even my old Aunt Maria Ignacia knew that I was going to Germany to study philosophy. I was to be a professor abroad, or if not a professor, an architect. There was no question any longer of a career in Spain; I was too old and too much expatriated by my English language and my American associations. On the other hand, I came to Avila with a sense of coming home and with the intention of always returning there. Official life would carry me out of Spain, as it had carried my father; but so long as he lived he would be my natural centre. While a student I should spend my longer holidays with him, and I vaguely foresaw, what has not proved altogether unlike the truth, that I should spend my old age, very much as he did, perhaps in Avila with another Don Pelayo for company.

The next day my father said we must go to see my cousin Elvira, daughter of his brother Nicolas, my godfather; she was now married and living in Avila. And married to whom? To Rafael Vegas, the same man who had been the husband of my other pretty cousin, the unfortunate Antoñita. In the interval of some fifteen years, naturally Rafael had not lived alone, but had married and buried his third wife. He was still the same peacock, though some of his plumes were now white, and when he wedded Elvira people shook their heads. He was a bluebeard and this poor young girl would die of childbirth within a year, like Antoñita,

76

and leave the old libertine, with his taste for dainty morsels, to gobble up some fifth victim. But the gossips this time were wrong. They didn't suspect the equal capacity of the fair Elvira, as yet unrevealed, for shedding yearly husbands. I have never heard of such a wealth of legal couplings as there were in her matrimonial circle. She was the fourth wife of her first husband, the second wife of her second, and the third wife of her third. She would remain each time childless, quietly smiling, and readier than ever to marry again.

Though short and fat, Elvira had a pronounced feminine charm. There was something calm, friendly, and sound about her person. Her clear white skin and no less clear brown eyes and soft curly brown hair gave her an air of neatness. She was *simplex munditiis*; and in spite of domestic duties, even at the times when she was poorest, she was always scrupulously clean. Her small hands moved nimbly and touched pleasantly; and she had a way of folding a scarf or shawl round her exuberant bosom that expressed happiness, grace, and almost humour. It was in the breast that she was most developed; the rest of her figure, though plump, seemed in comparison well-turned and almost tapering. She moved well; and when she was prosperous and suitably dressed—her third and last husband was a banker—she had the free and sure air of a lady. She ought to have been a lady, being born the daughter of an army officer who ought to have been a gentleman; and her Andalusian mother, whose name was Engracia or Grace, also had some pretensions to breeding or at least to luxury. But this only made her the more dissatisfied with her lot, her skin the yellower and her voice the shriller; and my maiden aunts, who resented her superior airs, used to say of their brother: *"Engracia le ha caído en gracia, y se ha desgraciado,"* which might be translated theologically by saying that Grace fell upon him and he was lost. The lady no doubt had a bad temper and could not forgive herself for being less brilliant than a sister of hers who had gone on the stage, who sang in light opera, married a rich man, became a widow when still young and good-looking, and lived luxuriously with her four children in Malaga, in an apartment like a *bonbonnière*, where I visited her in 1887. These were Elvira's "rich" relations, from whom she got her ideals of elegance and coquetry; yet by nature, like her father and mine and all true Castilians, she possessed a rather detached and sceptical philosophy, one that teaches us that all conditions are bearable, all dignities trumpery, and wisdom simply the gift of making the best of whatever is thrust upon us.

Rafael always had lived from hand to mouth, apparently prosperous but without any roots. His unexpected death left Elvira penniless, and she had to go and live with my father, in his poor man's house; for in spite of his own very modest means he was the stay and refuge of his whole family. This was the young widow's hibernation, and lasted several years. Whenever I came to Avila, I found her established at my father's as one of the family, at times with Susana, usually alone. She seemed resigned, disillusioned and cheerful. It was not at this time that she thought of perhaps marrying me. I was too young, a mere student from Germany, insignificant in comparison with her late pompous husband, who always took the lead in any circle, and knew by heart all the tricks of a country lawyer and an elderly ladykiller. But we got on very well together. I perceived that a year's life with Rafael, while it had left her without a shred of innocence, had neither disgusted nor corrupted her. She took the whole concealed side of life calmly, sensibly, without horror or curiosity; she had instinctively seen how tiresome it is; and we were able to talk about everything satirically, like two old cronies for whom the world has only a speculative interest.

She was not in those days without an earnest suitor, though she never accepted him, even as a *novio*. He was an excellent person, about forty-five years of age, but common; a cavalry captain who had risen from the ranks, whose name was Don Cándido. He was riding-master to the small garrison of the town, and gave me—as an indirect attention to Elvira—the only riding-lessons I ever took. They were of little use to me; I am not built for dancing or riding, and a foretaste of my necessary clumsiness at such things makes me avoid them. If I could ever have become good at them it would only have been, as in the case also of mathematics, if I had found an intelligent master who should have begun by explaining to me the *principles* of the thing, not an empirical practitioner like honest, dull Don Cándido who could only tell me to stick to the saddle and to go ahead.

But sticking to the saddle is not enough to please the ladies, and he never got ahead with Elvira. Somehow, however, she attracted the notice of a retired shop-keeper—let us call him merchant—a worthy and childless widower, who asked her to become his wife, as she sensibly did, foreseeing that he would soon leave her a little money, enough to make her independent. This happened almost at once; and then she took a small flat, in an *entresol,* overlooking the busiest street in the town. Sitting by her balcony, she was little above the heads of the passers-by. Everybody saw and admired her demurely sewing between her flower-pots; and she saw everybody and everything that passed, and through her maid or her own explorations she could learn everything that happened. It was a pleasant nest; and when I occasionally went to see her there, although we could hardly have the long unintentional conversations of the days when we lived in the same house, I became aware that she was considering the possibility of marrying me. She had no notion of geography or of foreign languages or foreign life; and seeing that I was well dressed and travelled about comfortably, she imagined she might live pleasantly in "America," that is, in Habana, on fifteen hundred dollars a year, which was then my salary. Probably she supposed that my family were rich and that I should have a share in their fortune.

It was not necessary for me to undeceive her on these points; my stay in Avila was short; and when I returned in a later year, I found that a far more desirable suitor had presented himself and been gladly accepted. He was her neighbour, and doubtless, from his own balconies on the first floor over his banking-house, he had watched her agreeable face at her window, and had been assured of her simple and quiet life. His second wife had recently died, leaving an infant in arms, his only child. What better mother than Elvira could be provided for it, or more blooming partner for himself?

In October 1905, I was in Avila, having a year's leave of absence from Harvard, and being on my way to Egypt, Palestine and Greece. The procession of *la Santa* passed Elvira's new house, and I was invited to see it from her windows. Two agreeable nieces of her husband's also were living there; the husband himself was gracious and well-spoken; we discussed the King's English marriage, then just announced, and I duly admired the fat and rosy baby. It was a picture of domestic happiness, dignity, and peace. But letters reached me that winter while I was in the East, announcing a rather strange and melancholy coincidence. Elvira had mysteriously fallen ill, and her husband also, and lying in separate rooms the two had died on the same day.

Elvira was not religious or romantic. Such a sudden fall of the curtain on a scene of decent well-being fits well with her person, her character, and her ideas. Her life had been thoroughly reasonable, frank and mediocre. After a Chinese fashion it was philosophical and sufficient.

The great event for me in Spain occurred upon my third return in 1887, when after my memorable first sojourn in England, and a month or two at Avila with my father and Elvira, I went to Gibraltar to meet Susana. That Susana should henceforth be in Spain (for I was sure she would never return to America, although she sometimes spoke of doing so "for a visit") weighted that centre of gravity decisively in my planetary system. It gave me an added reason for returning there often, and solved the problem of residence whenever I returned. For her, however, it was not a sufficient solution. She needed to be enthusiastic and she needed to be comfortable, and Spain was neither. Not that she had any feeling but affection for Spain, and loyalty to it even in those unhappy days; but now she was herself unhappy, and Spain didn't help her. Still, on the religious side the change of atmosphere was a relief; it removed the sense of tension under which she had so cruelly suffered; and this not merely externally or socially. I think that slowly, by living in Spain, her personal religious life was normalised, reduced to its healthy human function, and cleared of anxiety and bitterness.

On the social side, Susana was adaptable, and always took a healthy interest in the present. When in America she hadn't missed Spain, and now again in Spain she didn't miss America. Her good spirits in Boston, in the earlier days, had flowed from fun and comfort. When now she spoke of Boston society, she laughed at it for being so full of false pretenses and of insignificant points of pride. These were things that her Catholic discipline had taught her to put away. The only American memories that she seemed to idealise touched little luxuries and creature comforts: warm houses, bathrooms, table manners, ventilation, and *silver* knives, as she credulously called them, for the fruit. Her constitution was soft and frail, in spite of her robust appearance, and she suffered disproportionately from minor irritants; tobacco smoke, lights in the eyes, the crude scent of mutton, sourness even in good strawberries. She was weary; these trifles disturbed her physical peace, and made her seem less amiable than she was by nature. For in regard to people, though retrospectively critical enough, she was spontaneously sympathetic. Strangers, especially ladies, who saw her for the first time or had only occasional interviews with her, almost invariably liked her very much; but the value of such sympathy was only social, and left her daily life empty and dull. The fundamental difficulty came neither from Spain nor from America, neither from her friends nor her family. It came from the fact that she was thirty-six years old, and unmarried.

Between my father and Susana there was an old mutual affection and they attempted for a while to live up to it. For instance, Susana wished to make a pilgrimage to the tomb of Santa Teresa; but Alba de Tormes, where the saint is buried, was almost inaccessible, except on horse-back or, rather, on mule-back. There was a road of sorts, but no public conveyance, and a private carriage would have involved too much expense. My father, being a good pedestrian, was willing to walk there and back; and for Susana he conceived the plan of hiring a country waggon, with a mule and a *mozo*; a mattress could be spread out in the cart, which had a round canvas top: and there Susana could sit or lie down during the longer stretches. It was rickety, hard, and not very restful, and they would have to spend one night in whatever *posada* they could find at Alba; but they managed it. The excursion remained a memorable jaunt for him, and an act of piety or of penance for her: and there were no unpleasant effects except that in Avila she acquired the nick-name *la pelegrina*, which became capable of unkind interpretations.

For a few days, old affection and present good intentions could carry off the comedy between step-father and step-daughter; but it couldn't be kept up permanently. He was too old, crotchety, and poor; she was too much wedded to those religious opinions which directly or indirectly he was always attacking. Nor was there any need of keeping the thing up. She hadn't come to Spain in order to live with him, but rather with Doña Victorina and Mercedes. They had a flat in Madrid and a little house by the seaside, near Vigo, for the summer. Here there was no religious quarrel. Doña Victorina was pious, and Mercedes was more than pious: not only daily Mass and Communion, but apostolic labours in evening schools for workingmen in Vigo. Mercedes also had social position and, like Susana, had basked in the smiles of royalty; often visited the Infanta Isabel, and sometimes Queen Maria Cristina and even Queen Victoria Eugénie. Nevertheless, although in speaking to me both sides were naturally discreet, I could feel that between Susana and Mercedes there was no real sympathy, not even in religion. Mercedes was immensely spontaneous, pagan, superstitious, overflowing with devout sentiments, in diplomatic relations with the court of heaven even closer than with the court of Madrid. Susana was theological, instructed, theoretical; she justified her sentiments first and then, perhaps, she felt them. Mercedes was all initiative. In religion Susana had no initiative; she had sympathy only with things already afoot. She was at once imitative and satirical; because after mimicking involuntarily something that others were doing, her own disposition and intelligence reasserted themselves; so that she, like me, played a double part in her tragedy: she was one of the characters and also the chorus. And, unlike me, she had executive impulses that must have clashed with those of Mercedes. When she joined a movement she wanted to manage it. When she joined a family, if it were not possible or proper for her to rule it, she couldn't rest there. Cohabitation with the Escaleras was therefore never a real solution. Susana said that Galicia in summer didn't agree with her: the verdure and dampness brought on her New England "hay-fever." She preferred Avila. Yet Avila, secluded as it might seem, was a microcosm, with all the problems of a world. Besides the tension with my father, there was soon an open quarrel with Elvira. The two hadn't the same breeding; Elvira wasn't pious, she had been the wife of an old rake. Elvira on her side whispered things about Susana that oughtn't to be whispered and attributed motives that oughtn't to be attributed. It became impossible for my father's two guests to remain together. Elvira couldn't be sent away; she had nowhere to go, and no money. Her rich aunt in Malaga, on the first Christmas after Rafael's death, had sent a large box of raisins and other sweets to console her niece, who was so fortunate as to have a dear old uncle to live with in her widowhood; but on the second Christmas, when Elvira hoped to be invited by her dear rich aunt to go and live in Malaga, no present arrived and there was stony silence. It was therefore Susana, being independent, who had to leave. In winter, in any case, she was to join Doña Victorina and Mercedes in Madrid; the parting from my father had therefore nothing tragic about it; and Elvira automatically remained with him, uncriticised and blooming alone. But where should Susana spend the following summer? With Doña Victorina and Mercedes in Galicia, when she was a free American and preferred Avila? She wasn't going to allow an ill-bred, ill-natured woman like Elvira to upset her plan of life or control her movements. She would spend that following summer in Avila, in another house.

There were two quiet and agreeable elderly sisters, old friends of Susana's, whom we called *las de Madorell,* one of them a widow with two daughters. The elder daughter, Monserrat, had lately been married. They had room for Susana in their house and would be really glad of her company, much more entertaining than their own, and of the generous contribution she would make to their little budget. There was only one objection—a foolish one. *Las de Madorell* lived in the same street as Don Celedonio Sastre, an old flame of Susana's, now a widower. Evil tongues would say that she came to live in that street so that Don Celedonio should not be able to forget her existence and her proximity. Such nonsense had to be disregarded: but Providence had mysteriously designed the means of defeating such gossip before it arose. Monserrat unexpectedly died, leaving two little girls, one just born, the other a year older. Their grandmother, one of the Madorell sisters, would go to look after them, leaving still more room for Susana in the house, and would establish a sort of continuity, almost a union, between the Madorells' household and that of Monserrat's disconsolate husband.

This husband, now a widower, whose name was Bringas, thus became a second widower in Susana's immediate neighbourhood; and this to some purpose. Bringas was an army man and a professor in the Military Academy in Avila. Of the various Military Academies, this was the most modest, preparing cadets for the Commissariat; but this involved in the professors somewhat wider and more business-like knowledge than infantry or cavalry officers were expected in those days to imbibe: supplies and transport were at once scientific and commercial matters. Bringas accordingly had a rather wide acquaintance with international affairs, industrial as well as political; and from the first he had naturally found much to talk about with Susana, fresh as she was from twenty years' residence in the United States. I believe he was an intelligent as well as a kindly man; but all that I may have heard him say was obliterated in my mind by the image of his person and his extravagant gesticulation. He jumped about and waved his arms like a puppet on a wire: and he proved the absurdity of this, or the impossibility of that, with so much emphasis and victorious joy that you forgot entirely what the joy and demonstration were about. He was a thin, nervous man, I daresay very strong, with a thin black beard and bright black eyes: most lively, but most restless, and I should have thought most tiresome. Yet those who knew him well were greatly attached to him: and I think Susana liked him better, perhaps, than she did Celedonio, but also feared him more, and felt less secure in his presence. In Celedonio there were no possible surprises; he was older and thoroughly consolidated, in mind and body. Bringas was a jumping-jack, an electrical apparatus. Who could tell what he might do next?

The sympathy that grew up in these circumstances between Bringas and Susana was obvious to everybody: it was obvious to me whenever I saw them together: and it was known to Celedonio; so that the presence of Susana for one summer in his street, far from seeming an advance toward him on her part, proved a cause of jealousy. A passing cause: because before the next year Elvira had married her second husband; then Susana returned to live at my father's, and ultimately Bringas married his deceased wife's sister, who had always secretly cared for him. The storm in the Avila teapot had cleared, and Susana's future remained to be determined by undisturbed reason.

I call it reason because reason in my philosophy is only a harmony among irrational impulses; and the hesitating, much meditated, troubled course that Susana now took was rational only in that sense. She decided to marry Celedonio. In their difficult negotiations it was agreed that the wedding should take place *after* that of Celedonio's daughter, who was the eldest of his six children, and had been for some years at the head of his household. Obviously it would be unpleasant for her to be superseded there by a half foreign step-mother, with money of her own. The five boys wouldn't mind so much: they might even see the advantages of the change: they would have better food, more interesting talks, and perhaps a few lessons in English at home gratis. But Celedonio had the selfishness of lazy power. Without being ambitious or meddlesome, he was insensible to the desires of others. His daughter had a *novio* of whom he didn't approve. He desired her to marry another man whom she didn't like. He could not force her, of course; he was no tyrant; but he wouldn't allow her to marry the other man. His own marriage was therefore postponed or would have had to be given up; but that his dignity wouldn't permit. And he persuaded Susana to consent to their marriage *before* that of his daughter. If on trial, step-mother and step-daughter couldn't get on, that would be an added incentive for the girl to be reasonable and marry the man that pleased her father. And this wasn't the end of Celedonio's selfishness. Far from hastening his daughter's match when trouble began between the women at home, he put off any settlement. He liked to have his only daughter at home as well as his new wife. She could do him all sorts of little services, as of old, that were not to be expected of Susana; and she could look after the boys in the old slipshod economical way, and let Susana play the sultana, growing fat and indolent, in quite separate apartments. The result was that Celedonio found himself the master of two households, actually on two separate floors, his wife's and his daughter's. When definite disputes arose he settled them judicially, like a Roman father; and he pretended not to notice the daily friction, the estrangement, the grievances that grew worse every year. His daughter was condemned to die an old maid, and his wife never to feel identified with her new family or to secure their affection.

Only in the later years, after her stepdaughter had died and several of the boys were married, did Susana's position become less unpleasant. She had more money than at first and kept a part of it from her husband. This Yankee insistence on individual rights was a sort of revenge for not being accepted and appreciated as she deserved; but in the end it redounded to the advantage of Celedonio's family. In old age he became stingy, and he had always been insensible to his children's wishes and needs: the result was that they had hardly enough to live on. It was then Susana that came to the rescue; and the boys' wives were grateful. They called her *mamá,* as the boys had never been allowed to do by their sister: and they brought up the grandchildren to speak well of her and to respect her.

Celedonio was a landlord on a small scale, as well as a lawyer, and possessed a farm at easy riding distance from Avila, and a house in the town; but his chief occupation was to be agent for two or three greater landlords who had estates in the province and lived elsewhere. His house stood on the better side of the town, a little beyond the walls, and had a wide view over the *Valle de Amblés.* For me now it became a sort of summer home. Towns in these parts are cooler than the country. Thick stone walls and courtyards overhung with galleries protect from the merciless sun, while the keen mountain air blows through and keeps the lungs and the spirit fresh. Here my father's books, in their old bookcases, and various portraits painted by his hand, as well as odd things of my own, were collected in two little rooms to the left of the street entrance or *portal;* and this apartment was called *el cuarto de Jorge.* There I was entirely independent, with a door into the open court, and two barred windows on the square. To those bars sometimes in the early morning some passing peasant would tie his donkeys. I could hear the venders' cries, and the bells ringing not very melodiously for Mass, or tolling for the dead. I could also overhear various conversations of the passers-by, or of old women who stopped to gossip. I was in the old world; I might have been in the seventeenth century.

On the other side of the street entrance there was a large room, now a coach-house and lumber-room, that must have been originally the hall or countinghouse where the master sat and received his tenants or clients and carried on his business. In a restoration it would have made the best room in the house: an excellent library or billiard-room, according to the taste of the proprietor. Behind this lay the court, paved in large irregular stones and

stretching, on the ground floor, from wall to wall, the whole width
of the house; but the stone stairs, open to the air, led up on one
side to an overhanging gallery, supported by a few stone pilasters,
that ran round three sides of the court on the first floor, and left
only a central square open to the sky, with the tiled roof sloping
from all sides inward, so that during a heavy shower the water
came splashing and roaring down in four little cataracts upon the
stone pavement. This ground floor was not the ground floor at the
back: the sharp declivity of the land turned it into a second storey.
There was a central deep room, and two smaller rooms, one on
each side. The central one had a large alcove, with two beds,
where Celedonio and Susana slept: one of the smaller ones was his
office and the other her dressing-room. Upstairs the house was
again divided by the court into two distinct portions. In front,
looking out of the square, was a suite of five rooms, occupied by
Celedonio's daughter, and her aunt, her mother's maiden sister,
who had been left alone, and had become a member of this family.
She was a delicate, quiet person, and rather a blessing, since she
behaved well and kept her niece company. In the back part of this
floor were some new additions made by Celedonio: a large dining-
room with a 'splendid outlook, a kitchen, and several other rooms
for the boys and for the servants. We had breakfast—chocolate
and a large roll cut into long strips, and perhaps a glass of milk
in addition—each in his own room: and dinner was at two, or
whenever Celedonio had finished his business in his office. After
dinner the family dispersed immediately, and often Celedonio also
went downstairs to interview somebody who came on business.

Susana and I would usually sit for an hour or more *de sobre
mesa*, and if we were alone would sometimes drop into English.
But I didn't like this, unless reminiscences of Boston made it
appropriate. Susana's Spanish was better than mine, but her Eng
lish was worse, partly because of disuse, partly because she had
adopted indiscriminately all the ways of speaking that she had
heard, and some of them were dreadful. The best conversations
we had, however, were in the evening after supper, in the earlier

years. Supper was normally at half-past nine, sometimes later, and Celedonio would immediately go to bed and fall asleep. The boys went to the Mercado Grande, where the élite of Avila walked and sat on summer evenings, sometimes to the primitive music of the town band. Then Susana and I could sit by the open balcony in the *sala* admiring the extraordinarily brilliant starry sky, enjoying the cool of the night air, and discussing the past, the present, and the future. On the eternal we seldom touched. Her religious zeal had become wiser, she let God look after His own interests, and didn't worry any longer about other people's salvation.

The only entertainments for me during these many seasons in Avila were my long afternoon walks. At first Rafael, one of the boys, used to accompany me. He was sensitive to poetry, to re-ligion, and to the arts, without having much technical knowledge; but his feeling was genuine and uncontaminated by any passing fashion. In 1905–1906, when I was lecturing at the Sorbonne, I invited him to come and spend a month in Paris. He came: and I remember one day in the Louvre, when I pointed out some Luca della Robbia reliefs, his sudden interest, and the simplicity with which he took out a note-book and pencil, and made a sketch of one of the pieces, with a note of the colouring. "When I get back to Zorita" (his father's farm), he said, "I will make one like that." Later in Avila, however, I usually walked alone and reduced my-self to modest elderly circuits. The shortest and most obvious was to go round the city walls, down by the Rastro to the river, then up the old road skirting the north wall closely as far as San Vicente and then home by the Cathedral apse and the Mercado Grande. This walk—a question of less than an hour—had some-thing that especially recommends itself to my heart and lungs. The ups were all steep and short, the downs gradual and long drawn out. You were stimulated at moments to a little climbing, and you were insensibly propelled and aided in the long stretches. My father's favourite walk, up the *carretera* to the *alto de Vico* and back, had the disadvantage of a slight rise all the way out; also that of occasional dust and passing muleteers and pedestrians.

I preferred pristine solitude. Such was to be found by following the river downward, as far as the dam at the electric power station; it was a path amid great boulders, with varied effects of foreground and distance. But it meant coming uphill all the way home: and the same objection kept me from often choosing the road to Toledo, though the scene was pleasing and I came out into the country at once, without passing through the town. In the end I discovered something unexpected: that the foot-path along the railway line going toward Madrid made an excellent promenade. There were no trains either way at the hour when I went out; and the rocky slopes upward on one side, and the ravines downward on the other, gave you the sense of being in the mountains, as in fact you were. There were also more trees and grass than usual in these highland moors, where the earth is dressed prevalently, like the religious orders, in browns and greys. Avila, though it supports life, looks enough like a desert to symbolise the desert that the world is for the spirit, in spite of the crowd and the pressure there. In both you may come unexpectedly upon scattered flowers or herbs of the sweetest smell; and I treasured the double monition of that bare and austere landscape, and of those sombre yet glittering altars.

Those pleasant seasons in Avila were interrupted for me by the war; and when I returned in 1919, after five or six years' absence, though the places were the same, the persons were somewhat altered. We all were growing old. I in particular had been deeply affected, not only by the war but by a thorough review and digestion of all my English and American experience. I had written *Egotism in German Philosophy, Soliloquies in England* and *Character and Opinion in the United States.* Not being able to fix my thoughts on abstract matters I had read Dickens, and learned to love that humbler side of English sentiment and virtue. Without so much as asking for a reason my heart had been entirely on the English side during the war. At Avila, everybody's sympathies were entirely on the other side; and this antithesis rather disconcerted me. My Spanish too, from disuse, had become less fluent. There had been deaths in the family: the daughter, her aunt, and one of the sons. These things somewhat narrowed the field of talk and embittered it. I asked myself why I should still come here, if it were not to be a pleasure all round.

Yet there are attachments to persons and places that hold us even when they give us pain; and I found, at least the first year, a new pleasure here and a new attachment. Pepe, the youngest of the sons, had been married before the war and he now had two little boys, five and four years of age, who became my companions. Not for walks, naturally: but they would come into my room in the early afternoon and we would amuse ourselves painting pictures. When this vein was exhausted, I got a toy theatre, with various stage-settings and cardboard figures; and with my old box of water-colours at hand I was able to make other figures, and to reproduce one of the plays in which Susana had acted in her girlhood (our sister Josefina remembered the text) and also one or two Russian ballets that I had seen in Paris or London. We had one dress performance, to which the whole family was invited; and the preparations and rehearsals amused the little boys and amused me even more for days and days. These were not pastimes that could last long. When I returned in a later year the elder boy was not at home. He had been sent, probably for religious instruction, to an uncle, his mother's brother, who was a priest; and with the younger boy, Roberto, alone, we couldn't revive the old interest. But we read a book of Mother Goose, which they had; and although the child didn't learn much English, I learned sometimes how profound was the difference between modern English and Catholic breeding. Roberto was a sensitive and high-spirited boy; and when I translated for him the lines about Little Jack Horner and the Christmas pie, he felt the *fun* of it perfectly, until having stuck in his thumb and pulled out a plum, Jack Horner says, "What a good boy am I!" Instead of laughing at this, Roberto blushed, seemed a little embarrassed and doubtfully amused, as if he had heard something very improper. What a shocking, incredible thing, he thought, for anyone to say!

So deeply had the lesson of Christian humility penetrated into this society that it seemed scandalous even as a joke to imagine a greedy boy praising himself or congratulating himself. Even one's relations were never to be praised or boasted of. You might expatiate on how much you loved them: this was a source of care, a constant danger of great suffering, for you; it was not a virtue either in you or in those you loved. It was one of your trials, almost one of your sins. You were a bundle of imperfections. You might laugh or you might grieve; you never could have anything to boast of.

This boy Roberto had been so named after my brother, who had made at least two journeys into Spain, first with his whole family, then more wisely alone. He had been taken ill there; and stayed longer than he had intended. He had been with Mercedes to Galicia, and much delighted with her circle, in which, as I once counted it in Madrid, there were twenty-seven women and not one man. My brother Robert seemed a complete Yankee. He had no knowledge and no feeling of what Spain represents in history and in morals: but with Spanish women he returned, as it were, to a forgotten paradise. He was generically fond of the sex, of no matter what nationality, but Spanish women held him suspended in a special way between respect and desire; and far below his crude conscious level something in him responded to Spanish love and Spanish religion. This secret need—unknown even to himself—had inspired him with a great sympathy with Pepe, who wished to be married but was prevented by his father's opposition; and Robert succeeded in bringing Pepe's wedding about, partly by expostulating with Celedonio, going so far as to call him a tyrant, and partly by generous gifts of his own to help the young couple. It was in gratitude for this action of Robert's that they had named their second son Roberto.

My brother didn't live to see the destiny of his namesake; it was I who watched it from a distance with a special interest. Roberto was fond of books and all sorts of knowledge, reminding me of my boyish pleasure in geography and travels. He, like his brother, was also religious; they were among the first to catch the new wave of hope and enthusiasm for the moral regeneration of Spain. They joined the *Falange*, fought in the civil war, and Roberto, after being twice wounded, was killed at the end, within sight of victory. It is at once sad, bitter, and amusing to think how little my brother Robert, and the hundred million like him in America, could have understood this little tragedy, the fruit in one way of his overflowing good-will and kindness.

I watched all this, as I say, from a distance, because after Susana's death in 1928, there was little occasion or propriety in my imposing myself on Celedonio's family. I went that summer to Galicia, to see Mercedes and my sister Josefina; also to see something of that corner of Spain, which was new to me. I even passed through a corner of Portugal, taking the fast train from Paris to Oporto, and thence to Vigo by a secondary line; and on my way back I visited Santiago de Compostela, La Coruña, Leon and Palencia, studiously avoiding Avila, because I knew that the state of Celedonio's mind was unfavourable, and I wished to avoid unnecessary discussions. He was nearly ninety, full of crotchets, and bent on delaying the execution of Susana's will. He died, however, before the next summer; and then I did go to Avila, for the last time, to settle Josefina's affairs and also my own. This I managed without great difficulty. I gave my father's house, built by John Smith, to the Sastre brothers. For many years they had been collecting the rent of it for me, and this was only a small acknowledgment of their friendliness and of the prolonged hospitality of their family, which had been a cause of great joy to me. Besides, I persuaded Josefina to sign a letter—a formal will covering her American property had been signed in Vigo the preceding summer before the American Consul—asking her executors to give suitable legacies for life to Mercedes, the Sastre brothers, and some other friends of hers in Spain. Having thus burned my bridges and cleared my conscience in regard to business duties, I said farewell to Avila and to Spain, no doubt forever. I shed no tears. I retained within me all that I wanted or could ever now enjoy in Spain. I cut off only useless repetitions and disappointments.

My sister Josefina, who was seventy-seven years of age, died the next winter, peacefully, without pain, and without moral worries. She was not without a certain shrewdness in small matters, but vague and indifferent in most directions. After Susana's death, they found means of reconciling Josefina to the Church. Susana had been, curiously enough, the great obstacle to her sister's faith: Josefina didn't want to be dominated. But the ladies in Avila, who were pious without being aggressive or punctilious, won her over with soft words; and they told me that the Dominican who heard her confession said that he thought she had never committed a mortal sin in her life. Perhaps not. He saw that she was like a little child, docile or rebellious according to the tact of her elders, but irresponsible. Some lines from I don't know where stick in my mind for describing her perfectly:

> *Elle est morte et n'a point vécu.*
> *Elle faisait semblant de vivre.*
> *De ses mains est tombé le livre*
> *Dans lequel elle n'a rien lu.*

Susana, who had lived intensely and who had made brave, desperate ventures more than once in her day, could not hope for such a tranquil end. When time and death had solved the worst difficulties of her married life, and she might have expected to reach port in calm weather, a new and unforeseen trouble overtook her. Celedonio, who had never been considerate, became morose and intractable. At the same time, he became helpless. There arose a chronic resentment between them. The only comfort was that now his family was on her side; for it was the sons that suffered most from their father's obstinacy and niggardliness. Susana no longer slept in the other bed in Celedonio's alcove: one of his sons slept there, in case his father required help during the night. Susana had a bed in her dressing-room, which looked out into the broad country. She could sleep in a well-ventilated apartment. And she could keep her savings, as much as twenty thousand dollars, safe in a concealed drawer, unknown to her husband. And her thoughts could run—was it wicked to let them do so?—to the time when Celedonio would have disappeared, and she could restore the house next door—not this house, which had too many disturbing associations—to live in comfortably in her last days, with me and Josefina and the eldest of Celedonio's sons. Wouldn't he, I asked her, prefer to join one of his married brothers? No, said Susana, because in his brother's household he would have to pay his share of the expenses, while at his step-mother's he would get board and lodging for nothing.

Architectural dreams, as in our first days in Boston, again would bring us together. Should the court-yard have a glass roof? I said no. The duke of Valencia had put one into his restored palace because he was an Andalusian; and in Seville the *patio* was the family living-room in winter as well as summer, and they wished to be protected from the cold and rain. But in Avila no one would think of sitting in winter in a court-yard; the open air, on the south side of some great wall, was the place for sunning oneself: and a glass roof spoilt all the architectural effect and poetry of a *patio*. But Susana said the galleries would be terribly cold in winter for passing from one room to another. That, I retorted, could be prevented by glazing the upper galleries, leaving the court and lower gallery open to the sky. A glazed or even walled upper gallery was a characteristic and picturesque feature in mediæval houses. She might have that next door, and be both comfortably and artistically housed.

Celedonio must have surmised that, with various degrees of impatience, Susana, his sons and especially his sons' wives were waiting for him to die. Not a pleasing thought to hover over your pillow. And your retort in old age can hardly be to grow amiable and generous, so that everybody shall love you and wish you a long life. That is not feasible. The natural retort is to revenge oneself by growing more disagreeable and more miserly, and by straining every nerve to live longer than people expect. The sweetest triumph would be to survive all these younger people who wish to bury you. And Celedonio, as far as Susana was concerned, enjoyed this triumph. When I last said goodbye to him, "until next year," he shook his head, and muttered that he wouldn't survive that winter. He did survive it, but Susana, who was standing by and not thinking of dying so soon, did not survive it. She had never been really strong. At one time she grew enormously fat, then later lost flesh and seemed less unwieldy; but she suffered from physical and moral disharmonies in her nature, and never was or could be thoroughly resigned or content. The house next door was restored by one of her stepsons with her money; and the same pile of bank notes kept so secretly in her drawer served another stepson to restore the house she had lived in for thirty-five years, in comparative shabbiness and discomfort. She and I never had our architectural domicile together; and she never enjoyed the sense of having found her true place in the world and of having won the esteem and gratitude of those who surrounded her. The bar sinister, as it were, of divided allegiances and of incompatible demands always cut across her fairest prospects.

Susana was a Sturgis. Like many of the Sturgises she had good looks, good humour, enthusiasm, love of society, and love of fun; and like the best of them, like her Aunt Sarah, she had also an intrepid instinct of leadership and could direct her passionate interest to some ideal and public end, in her case, towards the Catholic Church. This was not an effect of special intellectual or mystical insight into religion; the Sturgises were not naturally religious. It was an effect of contagion: she easily caught any ambient enthusiasm, and held to it more innocently perhaps and longer than those from whom she caught it. At the same time, she needed social support and sympathy. It would have been agony for her to have been alone with Allah. In order to flourish she required benign and congenial influences. Had these been more prevalent in her life she would have been universally loved and admired. Her mind would have been enlarged and refined; whereas in her continually difficult position she could hardly avoid the irritability and the unjust judgments of the unsatisfied. Yet this ran counter to her nature; I, to whom she had always shown her best side, could feel the warm affection beneath her partisanship, and the comedy behind her illusions. She couldn't bear to let the good and the beautiful slip by unrealised. Hence her impulse to dominate and to manage. That which grieves me now in her destiny is not so much what she missed as what she suffered. It is a shame that she should have suffered, when she was created to love, to laugh, and to enjoy.

CHAPTER V

YOUNGER HARVARD FRIENDS

ONE EVENING in the autumn of 1889, when I was stammering my first lectures in philosophy, there was an unexpected knock at my door in Thayer Hall: and on opening, I saw before me a young man of middle height, with dark hair and a smiling mouth, who said: "My name is Barlow, and my mother has asked me to come and see you." Two simple facts, baldly stated, with an air betwixt sheepishness and mockery, and conveying everything that I needed to know. Here was a Sturgis. His mother, whom we called Nelly Barlow, was the prettiest of "Aunt Sarah's" four daughters, and had married a rough diamond, General Barlow, fresh from the Civil War. The young man was Bob, their eldest son. I don't remember the rest of our conversation that evening, but we had no lack of subjects, knowing perfectly who and what we both were, and being equally at home at Harvard. I perceived at once that Bob had an acute, realistic mind; he didn't mince matters; and his way of talking might have seemed brutal but for a certain background of refinement and indifference that kept it from being conceited or aggressive. We are all fools and poor devils, he seemed to be saying, and we might as well put up with that fact.

Some years later, I saw his father in their house in New York, where after looking at his son's head and at mine where the hair was getting thin, he observed dryly: "The trouble with you young men is that you are rotten before you are ripe." A conspicuously pretty mother and a conspicuously gruff father explained the character of their first born. Bob was a satirical lover of the frail sex and frequented all levels of female society, approaching the dear creatures with a cold eye but with gallant inclinations. He allowed himself no exclusive passions, and remained a bachelor all his life. He particularly liked Paris, the French language and the French stage, about which he knew more than does the ordinary tourist. He was rather well read, with a relish for the sayings of wits, rakes, and cynical philosophers. Boldness pleased him in thought and in war, no less than in love; any man of character had his respect who dared speak the truth and shame the hypocrites. With this taste, sharpened and fed by legal practice, for he became a lawyer, went a certain gentleness of aspect and manner, equable, lazy, and a bit sleepy. You saw in him the child of a beautiful woman who lived to be over ninety; and he himself, though not positively good-looking, had the placidity of a privileged person, round whom everything was expected to revolve without demanding from him any special effort. He led a life of pleasure with apparent indifference, not to say melancholy, and he might have appeared somewhat weak or disappointed had he stood alone.

But Bob Barlow never stood alone. He was one of a pair, like statuettes for the mantelpiece. His mate, however, was no shepherdess, but a big, heavy, jolly man named "Swelly" Bangs, once centre of the 'Varsity football squad, and later an imposing judge. Nobody spoke of Barlow and Bangs; everybody said Bangs and Barlow, as if they had been a firm of lawyers in Dickens, and Bangs the senior partner. But, though both lawyers, they were not partners, Barlow having lived at first with his parents in New York, while Bangs was faithful to Boston. Bangs was simply the greater weight, the more obvious presence, with the more emphatic voice and the more aggressive opinions. What in Barlow was an innuendo turned in Bangs into a crushing dictum, as if he were about to sentence the prisoner to the gallows. Both friends had the mentality of the eighteenth century, and Bangs might have reminded one of Dr. Johnson, save that he banged most softly, with an air of the fine gentleman; for "Swelly" was a man of fashion. My first sight of him was when I was sitting in my lecture-room, waiting for the usual seven minutes to elapse before beginning; and, the place being almost empty, I noticed a new person dressed in a yellow Norfolk-jacket with a large plaid come in and deliberately choose a seat at the back of the room. He then produced a small leather ink-stand and *a quill pen* for the improbable purpose of taking notes. I don't think he came again; but on mentioning the apparition, I was informed that "Oh, yes, he was well-known. It was Swelly Bangs." Neither he nor Barlow was especially my pupil, or much given to technical philosophy. The bond between them and me was of another kind. It was what I might call the sporting mind, unbiased intelligence, spreading freely from youthful curiosity to the interests of the world in general, including the adventures of the philosophers: a sporting mind found in the old wits, in Montaigne and Voltaire, in Hobbes and in Dr. Johnson, but seldom found anywhere nowadays, least of all in America.

Bangs and Barlow sometimes took me to supper at a club they belonged to called popularly *The Spee* and officially the Zeta Psi. The dining-room resembled an old-fashioned ship's cabin, narrow, low, with sides and ceiling all panelled in wood, and a cushioned bench running round the wall. A narrow long table occupied the space between, so that dishes had to be passed along from hand to hand till they got back to the lower end of the table: and I think there were nautical lanterns for the lights, and other little suggestions of the sea. A pleasant setting for my fancy: confinement and comradeship in the midst of a boundless wilderness, and freedom of mind without the peril of losing one's physical balance. The company, the tone, the yarns, and the songs, if not literally nautical, yet had the mannish character proper to a band of young spirits escaping, in sport or in earnest, from the conventional world to sea or into the wilds. Bangs himself used to recite a whaling story, always called for on these occasions, which proved how a ritual gains by repetition. Everybody knew it by heart, and sometimes recited it in chorus. It was called, "Cap'n Sims, thar she blows!" It was full of dialect and local colour; and I still remember Captain Sims' praises of salt pork. Other victuals,

he said, leave you half hungry, but salt pork "lays there a-nourish-
ing of you for days and days." The supper, however, didn't con-
form to this ideal, but was apt to include scalloped oysters and a
welsh rarebit, with excellent drinks, both hot and cold. It was a
somewhat freer and rougher society than I had known in my own
college days, but I liked it immensely and didn't feel out of place
in it. Being a little older than the others and a teacher in the
College, I wasn't expected to contribute to the entertainment, nor
had I any gifts in that direction. I might sometimes say a *bon mot*,
but I could never tell a good story. Nature thus helped me to be
discreet in all my relations with the younger people, and to preserve a certain propriety of language which the youngsters respected, and didn't seem to dislike. At any rate, I was asked
repeatedly to *The Spee,* where Bangs and Barlow were always my
hosts. My position in these undergraduate circles was like that of
the prefect in *"Le Monde ou l'on s'ennuie,"* then a well-known
comedy, when the duchess, going in to dinner on the prefect's
arm, sighs that he won't be able to tell tales about the government,
and he replies, "No, Madame, but I may listen to them." So I
was able to listen to "Cap'n Sims" and to much else, without
either forgetting my status or spoiling the fun.

The Bangs family had a country house near Wareham, in the
flat sandy region of Cape Cod, and during one Easter vacation
"Swelly" had an angling party there, in which I was included;
for though I had never held a rod in my hand, and never meant
to, I was notoriously content with looking on; and the nominal
duty was assigned to me of opening the baskets and laying out the
food for the luncheon in the woods. The woods are rather meagre
and scrubby in Cape Cod; but there was moss and rock enough
by that sluggish little stream to sit down with comfort, and trees
high enough to produce an illusion of being embowered. And we
camped out pleasantly at the house, which was closed except for
a caretaker, and cooked our own food by a roaring wood fire after
our exhilarating day in the fresh air. It was on this occasion that
I wrote some lines on *Cape Cod,* of which the poet William

Moody said that there for once I had been inspired. But that inspiration came only by the way, as on returning we skirted a beach in the gathering twilight. Cape Cod in general has the most cheerful associations in my mind.

For here too, at Cotuit, lived the Codmans; and it had been in the summer of 1889 that I had stayed there, forming an affectionate friendship with the whole family, and in particular with Julian, the youngest son. The mother, whom we called "cousin Lucy," was a daughter of the great Russell Sturgis of London, by his first marriage; and although she had married a Bostonian, a somewhat English atmosphere permeated the household, its habits, its speech, and its sentiments. The family were Episcopalians, though not yet Anglo-Catholics. This was not really backsliding towards superstition, as Old Boston might think; everybody knew that Bishop Brooks was as liberal as any Unitarian, only nicer; and Julian, though apparently merely a rather short but well-built and good-looking young man, with excellent unaffected manners, had imbibed secret religious feelings; not so secret, however, that I wasn't perfectly aware of them. I liked those feelings. They were ballast, good for a young man of family who might otherwise dance too lightly on the summer waves.

The always agreeable Julian also had a feeling for poetry, which (like me, if less speculatively) he merged in religion: poetry, especially of the Victorian sort, perspicuous, highly aesthetic, elevating, yet disillusioned. That disillusion should be elevating was nevertheless a mystery; because after all it wouldn't do not to play the game. Pessimism was allowed when it was sincere, but the matter simply remained in suspense for a solution to be found later. With this happy turn of mind, Julian became the life of my "poetry bees," as he called them, when half a dozen of his friends would come to my room in Stoughton in the evening, to beer or hot Scotch whisky, and poetry: most often Keats, but often also Shelley, or Shakespeare's sonnets and songs. Without Julian's tact and fidelity the others (except Warwick Potter) would hardly have proved constant: but he gave the thing such

a good start and chose the participants with so much tact that
the pleasant practice lasted for years. Harvard social distinctions,
not founded on wealth, breeding or attainments, had to be understood and respected if anything of this kind were to be "a success."
For instance, I had a friend who was himself a poet, exceptionally
cultivated, and educated by his father (an unemployed teacher)
to perfection: Joe, or, as he preferred to call himself, Trumbull
Stickney. I once tried to introduce him into our readings; but no,
it wouldn't do. Julian confidentially informed me that "the others
didn't like him." Why not? Because he had mentioned the sunset
and called it "gorgeous." I understood that he was too literary
and ladylike for Harvard: and I myself found him more com-
panionable later in Paris, where my memory prefers to place him.

Many years later, in 1910–1911, I revived these poetry readings,
but almost as if they were a university "seminar." We met in the
afternoon, regularly once a week, and read only Shelley from
beginning to end, except *The Cenci*. Julian's mantle, on that occasion, had fallen on the worthy shoulders of Conrad Aiken. He
was the soul of the party; and we were too sensible, and too intent
on our poet, to note particularly who took part. Friendship was
not a prerequisite or a necessary result: for me the thing had an
ulterior use, in that it led me to write my essay on Shelley.

Julian was a great comfort to me in those earlier days; reconciled me to being again at Harvard without my old friends, and
gave me fresh information, judicious and never uncharitable,
about things and persons in that little world. He had no fads, no
vices, no prejudices, no faults. A little negative, you might say:
and description can hardly do him justice. He was amiable, but
having no special gifts, he lost distinction as he lost his youth. To
have remained at forty or fifty as socially perfect as he was at
twenty would have required one artificial aid: plenty of money.
He would have known how to combine, in a generous establish-
ment, material, intellectual and social pleasures; his legal profession would not have left him without sufficient leisure and his
house would have been a Mecca for all his friends. Even as things

were, I was always happy in his company. Our nominal relationship through the Sturgises covered a real affinity. He was a young man of the world, and made no bones of differences in age, or nationality. We laughed at the same things, and we liked the same things. What more is needed for agreeable society?

On the same sandy coasts of Cape Cod I repeatedly visited another young friend, Cameron Forbes, at Naushon, an island in Buzzard's Bay that belonged to his grandfather, Mr. John Forbes, a personage who had played an important part, financially, in the remote times of the Mexican War and the annexation of Texas and California. "Cam," as he was called, inherited from that grandfather, as well as a prospective fortune, an aptitude for affairs and for public life. He was not a youth to waste his time lounging in clubs, nor was he particularly absorbed in books; when he had a free day he would escape from Cambridge to his family farm or estate or settlement in Milton, where there were horses and woods and crops and buildings to inspect and to look after. At Harvard his most urgent occupation was football, not only the practice of it but the theory, and he eventually became coach to the 'Varsity eleven, which that year, by what seemed a miracle, won the Yale Game.

All this sounds rather remote from my meditative idleness; but Cam had another grandfather. He was also the grandson of Emerson. That heritage was no less real in him, though less apparent: or rather, it appeared in him negatively, as a saving check or divine inhibition. It kept him absolutely removed from playing the rich young man. Simplicity, rusticity, hard work, and public duty held him fast bound; yet as with Emerson so in him, this severity was practical more than imaginative. Imaginatively he could escape from business as gladly as, in life, he fled from luxury. There was no moral hesitation, no temptation to be soft: his whole life, in spite of uncertain health, was devoted to affairs, to politics, to administration: he was at one time Governor of the Philippine Islands; and I heard that in his old age, still a bachelor, he lived in his grandfather Forbes' house in Naushon

surrounded by his brothers' families, and most affectionately playing the patriarch. Nevertheless, transcendentally, I think he was
haunted by the suspicion that all this ado was terribly unnecessary, just as football, if you think of it, is terribly unnecessary;
and instigated by that qualm, he would sometimes draw me
aside, and talk about rather intimate matters. He was not one of
my little circle: but trusted that my experience and philosophy
would enable me to understand in him that which he himself
hardly understood.

One day, for instance, he showed me some verses of his about a
young man dreaming that two goddesses, Life and Death, appeared
to him and offered him their respective gifts: a sort of Puritan
Judgment of Paris. The young man listens to their respective
boasts and respective promises, and then says: I will choose Life,
but on one condition: that I may afterwards reverse my judgment,
and choose Death.

The verses were not well composed, and I doubt that Cam has
written any others; but the thought was so original, so wise, and
so courageous, that nothing in Emerson has ever pleased me
more. Think what an incubus life would be, if death were not
destined to cancel it, as far as any fact can be cancelled. That is
the very image of hell. But natural life, life with its ascending
and descending curve, is a tempting adventure; it is an open path;
curiosity and courage prompt us to try it. Moreover, the choice
must have been made for us before it can be offered; we are
already alive, and a whole world of creatures is alive, like us. The
first question is therefore what this world may bring to light, for
others and for ourselves, so long as it endures. Therefore the
preference for life is, as Cam felt, a duty, as well as a natural
sporting impulse; but it is a conditioned preference, and something
deeper in us than any casual prompting transcends that preference
and is fortified by being able to transcend it.

Various traits, major and minor, belonging to Cam Forbes were
appropriated by me for the hero of *The Last Puritan*. In the first
place, the relation to his father, the atavism of Puritan blood as-

serting itself, affectionately and kindly, but invincibly, against a
rich father, a sportsman, and a man in whose life there was
something vague and ineffectual. I didn't know Mr. William
Forbes well, nor much about him; but he was present and played
the host the first time I went to Naushon. We had champagne
every day for dinner; something so entirely contrary to Cam's
instincts or possibilities, that when I went to Naushon the second
time, with a party of young men from Harvard, Cam commis-
sioned one of us to provide the drinks: even to think of them or
order them repelled him. Yet it was a purely private and inward
protest: his conscience allowed him to pay for the drinks of others.
But my Oliver is no portrait of Cam or of anyone else, although
many of the details are drawn from life in various persons. I meant
the divine vocation in Oliver, though unrecognised, to be radical
and devastating; there was nothing so definite in Cam, who was
able to live the expected life and to make a "success" of it. And
I also gave Oliver a better education and more ability than Cam
ever had, and a greater sensitiveness to the equal rightness of the
gay world and the religious world from which his own destiny
had cut him off.

Here are three young men (excluding Bangs) who were grandsons, not as we all are, but essentially, so that being grandsons
dominated their characters and their whole lives. In other words,
they illustrated the decline of an age—the age of the great merchants. They were in one sense its ripe fruits, but in another sense
they marked the dissolution of that economy, its incapacity to
maintain itself for more than three generations. Two of my
friends never married—a rare and almost discreditable thing in
their world—and the third died rather young and left, I believe,
only one child. Either their fortune was inadequate, or their
virtue was inadequate, or their health and stamina were inade
quate. Gently, or sadly, or cynically, they had to bow themselves
off the stage. But this decline regards only a phase of society,
not the life of society as a whole, which in New England was
growing richer and more vigorous as it passed out of the period

of great merchants into that of "big business" and was merged in
the vast American vortex. These grandsons, these essential de-
scendants, couldn't merge in it. They were not hardy enough,
not crude enough, too well aware of what they would miss. They
were not Babbitts.

Apart from any possible affinity to Babbitt, good sense and good
nature (as in Bangs) kept the majority of well-bred Bostonians
from being merely grandsons; and in some there was pure individual spontaneity and the certainty of having a fixed vocation.
This was the case at that time with another young friend of mine,
Howard Cushing. When an undergraduate he was already a
painter, and sure that he would never wish to be anything else.
The whole world was there before him for a model and he would
never tire of catching poses and distinguishing colours. He was
not poor, he spoke French fluently (his mother belonged to an
old French family in Louisiana), and he was at home in all
countries, but never happier than in his own. He loved what he
called the *fearless look* of Americans; and his nature was so
aristocratic (like that of Thomas Jefferson) that he could feel
and actually be perfectly free, even in a democracy. What the
crowd did and what the crowd thought was a splendid subject to
observe, if not to paint, like scenes from the French Revolution
or the martyrdom of early Christians: it was all delightfully full
of colour and character. Yet what in the end he painted with most
pleasure was the wonderful golden-red hair of his young wife
and of his little children. He was domestic, all affection and
simplicity, and something of his painter's art seemed to overflow
into his surroundings, wherever he might be, and turn them into
a picture.

I should hardly have known these younger men, or known them
so intimately, but for what we called "the club." In my undergraduate days three of my best friends, Ward Thoron, Herbert
Lyman, and Boylston Beal, who ought to have been invited to
join some club, such as that to which Bangs and Barlow later
introduced me, found themselves left out in the cold; and it

occurred to them to found a new club of a socially superior kind, less popular perhaps, and less athletic, but more distinguished. They invited me to join them; but clubs with assessments and inevitable incidental expenses were then beyond my slender means. That club had now amply fulfilled its promise; it had gathered together stray young gentlemen not duly appreciated by their contemporaries but interesting in themselves, some rich, others clever, still others simply agreeable. Julian Codman, Cam Forbes, and Howard Cushing belonged to this club. It then (1890) occupied a wooden house in Mount Auburn Street, and was called officially the Delta Phi, or more familiarly "The Gas House," because all its windows would be lighted up at once by the electricity that was then a novelty; so that it was called "The Gas House" because of the absence of gas. Yet the nickname stuck, and could be interpreted to refer to the brilliancy of the members' minds, or the vanity of their speech. My contemporary, Beal, who had spent some years in Europe, was still studying at the Law School, and came daily to this club; and I suspect that it was he that suggested that I might now be made an honorary member. This was done, and I soon became an *habitué,* and picked up many a stray meal there, not having a regular eating place. There was another graduate, besides Beal, to keep me in countenance, Billy Woodworth, who was an Assistant at the Agassiz Museum, and an excellent cook. He would sometimes preside at supper, producing a dish of his own invention, and his conversation opened to most of us new perspectives, scientific and social, for he was a Californian of the freest type.

It was at the club that I formed the most unclouded and heartfelt of my American friendships, that with Bob and Warwick Potter. Of Bob I will speak later; he was in the class of 1891, and in his last year at Harvard he was preoccupied with his future. He was as much an architect by vocation as Howard Cushing was a painter, and they were both full of the studies they were about to make in Paris, at the Beaux-Arts or at Julien's. But Warwick, who was in the class of 1893 and died at the end of that year, was for the two previous winters my constant companion, and also pupil; and it was at the club, during our poetry-readings in my room, and on our walks that I insensibly came to think of him as a younger brother and as a part of myself. I didn't know how much attached to him I was, until I heard the unexpected news that he had died on board Edgar Scott's yacht in the harbour of Brest. He had been terribly seasick, and the seasickness had provoked an attack of cholera that had proved fatal. It seemed a new kind of blow, not violent, not loud, but strangely transforming. A gradual change due to many converging causes was going on within me. A twelvemonth before, my sister Susana had been married; that summer, my father had died; and the death of Warwick now came to accentuate the effect of these mutations and to make me aware of their meaning for my spiritual life. I shall return later to this my *metanoia.* Nothing apparently was much changed in my surroundings, opinions or habits; yet the public world was retreating to a greater distance and taking on a new and more delicate colouring, as if by aerial perspective. I realised that it was not my world, but only the world of other people: of all those, at least, and they were the vast majority, who had never *understood.*

I have already said something about Warwick in comparing him to my early friend Bayley: they were both good, or rather loved and understood the Good; for they were both too young to have been tried in the furnace and proved to be pure gold. But I felt that they were pure gold. There was an important element in Warwick, however, that didn't appear in Bayley: Warwick was full of laughter. Now laughter, as I have come to see in my old age, is the innocent youthful side of repentance, of disillusion, of understanding. It liberates incidentally, as spiritual insight liberates radically and morally. Susana also was full of laughter; it was the deepest bond between us. By laughing together we could erase the traces of any divergence or failure of sympathy. At the same time, Susana, like Bayley and Warwick, was devout; this marked their sensitiveness to the Good, their capacity to worship. These were the two prerequisites, in my conception, to perfect friendship: capacity to worship and capacity to laugh. They were the two windows through which the mind took flight and morally escaped from this world.

Warwick was not clever or specially good at his lessons: had he become a clergyman, as he rather expected, his scholarship would have been his weak point, and his theological ideas would have remained vague and verbal. Yet he was very well educated after the manner of ladies (which was rather the Groton manner); he had heard of everything, knew the points of the compass in morals and history, and had good taste in English literature. He also had good taste in choosing his friends and in judging them: and his intimates were not of his own type: they were not good pious boys, but captains of crews and owners of yachts: young men who had experience far beyond his own innocence. He was not out of place in their society, as he was not in that of his masters at Groton or in mine. Though young for his age in experience, he was intellectually alert and without prejudice and laughingly open to every interesting fact or idea—a trait that youth ought to possess but that is really the sign of a rare maturity. You could sit with him by the fire over a mild whiskey and soda, until the early hours, discussing Falstaff and Prince Henry, or the divinity and humanity in Christ, or the need of arms to give strength to letters. Both are needed; and the whole world is needed, and a complete view of life, to give light to friendship.

These relations of mine with younger spirits were all cut short by early separations. That was in the nature of things, because friends should be contemporaries. But I was divided from my contemporaries by initial divergences of race, country, religion, and career; and in spite of those barriers, my old friends kept their place in my affections and interest to the end. Modern life is not made for friendship: common interests are not strong enough, private interests too absorbing. Even in politics, colleagues are seldom or never friends. Their ambition, being private and not patriotic, divides instead of uniting them. Nevertheless, I continued to have young friends, very nice young friends, all my life: a little ghostly and evanescent, but agreeable. As widowers proverbially marry again, so a man with the habit of friendship always finds new friends. I had many more at Harvard: I will speak of some of them among Americans in Europe, since it was usually in Europe that our acquaintance could first become companionship; but it would be monotonous to repeat story after story, all with the same moral, and in the same landscape. Harvard had nothing essentially new to offer or to awaken within me, after I returned from King's College, in 1897: the following fifteen years that I remained a professor were a somnambulistic period, interrupted only by the waking dream of a journey to Egypt, Palestine and Greece. Persons yielded in interest to places; and having chosen a place for the time being, I lived as best I could with the human souls that inhabited it. Not at all in bitterness; not with any painful sense of disappointment. My old age judges more charitably and thinks better of mankind than my youth ever did. I discount idealisations, I forgive onesidedness, I see that it is essential to perfection of any kind. And in each person I catch the fleeting suggestion of something beautiful, and swear eternal friendship with that.

CHAPTER VI

BOSTON SOCIETY

WHEN in the year 1858 my mother heroically fulfilled her promise to her late husband and first went to live in Boston, she knew what she was doing, for she had spent some months there two years before and had made the acquaintance of all the Sturgises and their friends. And yet I think she had expectations that were never realised. If not for herself—since she had lost all interest in society —at least for her children, she pictured a perfect amalgamation with all that was best in Boston. This amalgamation never took place. I have described the difficult position that my sister Susana found herself in, and her ultimate return to Spain; and my brother Robert, though a thorough American in all externals, never made a place for himself in good Boston society. This society, in my time, was on the one hand clannish, and on the other highly moralised and highly cultivated. The clannishness was not one of blood: you might almost say that all the "old families" were new. It was a clannishness of social affinity and habit; you must live in certain places, follow certain professions, and maintain a certain tone. Any adaptable rich family could easily enter the charmed circle within one generation. Money was necessary, not in itself but as a means of living as everybody else did in good society; and those who became too poor fell out within one generation also. As to the other characteristic of being cultivated and high-principled, it was not indispensable for individuals already in the clan; but it was necessary to the clan as a whole, for a standard and a leaven. I suspect that the lack of those qualities may have dissolved the society that I speak of, and allowed it to become indistinguishable from the flowing mass of the rich and fashionable all the world over.

Conversation in society, for me at least, was almost exclusively with ladies; but whenever I found myself by chance among elderly men, as for a while after dinner, I became aware of living in a commercial community. Talk reverted from banter to business worries, if not to "funny stories." The leaders were "business men," and weight in the business world was what counted in their estimation. Of course there must be clergymen and doctors also, and even artists, but they remained parasites, and not persons with whom the bulwarks of society had any real sympathy. Lawyers were a little better, because business couldn't be safeguarded without lawyers, and they often were or became men of property themselves; but politicians were taboo, and military men in Boston non-existent. Such persons might be occasionally entertained, and lauded rhetorically in after-dinner speeches; but they remained strangers and foreigners to the inner circle, and disagreeable to the highly moralised and highly cultivated Bostonian.

My contacts with this society were neither those of a native nor those of a visiting foreigner; nor could they be compared with my relation to Harvard College, where I was as much at home as anybody, with a perfectly equal and legal status. In order to have slipped no less automatically and involuntarily into Boston society, I should have had to go to a fashionable school, and my family would have had to occupy the position that I imagine my mother had dreamt of. As it was, I skirmished on the borders of the polite world, and eventually limited myself to a few really friendly families. Yet at first my lot fell, as was natural, within the circles of the Sturgises, especially of the children and grandchildren of Russell Sturgis of London.

In the summer of 1889, when living at my mother's at Roxbury and preparing my first course of lectures, I received an invitation to spend a few days at Manchester-by-the-Sea, with Russell Sturgis, Jr., and his family. I had never seen this elderly cousin, or any of his younger children: only once, many years ago, his eldest son.[1]

From Susana's satirical gossip of years before I had learned something about her cousin Russell. He was very Evangelical, distributed tracts entitled "Do you love Jesus?" and would send us Christmas cards—he never came to see us—wishing us joy and "one more year of leaning upon Jesus' breast." There was always some religious motto printed on his note-paper, which once happened to be "Ye are bought with a price"; and he having inadvertently written to Judge Gray on that paper, his letter was returned as a libel by the insulted magistrate. Apart from his evangelical work "Cousin Russell" appeared to have no occupation; and he was known to have spent the winter at Manchester-by-the-Sea for economy, which precluded daily attendance to business, if he had any. He may also have thought that on moral grounds, as a discipline and a tonic, a winter in the bleak country might be a good thing. The "kindred points of heaven and home" might there seem more precious than ever. We are always so near the abyss, and the wintry ocean might remind him of it. But why suddenly ask me to stay at his house, when he had never seen me and there was no real bond between our families? Had he heard that I was about to begin teaching at Harvard? If I were the right sort, might I not prove a useful acquaintance for

[1] This had been in the year 1876, when I was twelve years old. Robert and I had gone to Philadelphia to see the Centennial Exhibition. I remember only two things seen in Philadelphia, both architectural: the Fine Arts Building and the odd features of the typical Philadelphia houses: the white wooden shutters outside, and the ingenious arrangement of the stairs, making a bridge between the body of the house and a long wing behind, entered from the landing. The stairs could be lighted through a large window at the side, and the wing would supply various rooms, the dining-room especially, half-way between one storey and another of the house proper. For some reason, on our return, Robert wished to stay in New York. Young Russell Sturgis, 3rd, then nineteen years old, offered to look after me on the way home. We travelled by the Sound Boat—another interesting discovery in construction—a vast flat-bottomed steamer with a hall in the middle, surrounded by galleries and rows of little doors to private cabins. If we had only been quadrupeds, we should have fancied ourselves in Noah's Ark.

his younger sons, who were younger than I? And if I were not the right sort, why shouldn't he prove a saving influence over me?

When I turned up, I don't know what his first impression may have been; he and the whole family were certainly very kind. They seemed to accept me as an adopted relative. But gradually my defects must have become evident. No, I didn't swim, and I'd rather not take a dip in the sea before breakfast, as he and the boys did every morning even in winter. I didn't say so, but it cost me an effort to be shaved and dressed in time for the inevitable family breakfast. Lazy, soft, luxurious young man, and a *poor* young man, too, which makes vice so much worse and so much less excusable! However, these thoughts were as yet only in embryo. I got down to breakfast in time—a very nice breakfast, all sorts of hot things, not unwelcome when one has got up early—but after it there was a strange, awkward silence; everyone was standing up and no one leaving the room except to move into the drawing-room, which was separated only by a screen. The servants now came in, and stood uncomfortably in a corner. There were to be family prayers! They were *after* breakfast, as "Cousin Russell" afterwards frankly explained, because if they had been *before* breakfast, everybody would have been late or would have missed prayers altogether; but after breakfast, there you had them all, and no escape. Filled and soothed as I was by that abundant oatmeal, I rather liked the idea of prayers. I should have a peaceful quarter of an hour, speculative, digestive and drowsy. Chairs, big and little, were arranged in a circle round the room. In lieu of ecclesiastical objects, the broad sea and sky were visible through the long open windows. We might enlarge our thoughts, while "Cousin Russell" read a chapter of the Bible, not at all in a clerical voice, but familiarly and dramatically, to bring out the good points, and make us feel how modern and secular it all really was. The book closed, he rose and we all rose automatically to attention—he had been a major in the Civil War—we executed a sharp right-about-face, fell on our knees, and buried our faces in the warm chairs where we had been sitting. He recited, and the rest half murmured, the Lord's Prayer, with some other short things from the Prayer-Book, and a benediction. Then we all rose again, the servants disappeared, and a programme of healthy pleasures was announced for the rest of us for the morning. In the afternoon there would be an excursion and in the evening (not preannounced) there were to be parlour-games.

Never having been in an army, in a nursery, or in an Evangelical family, I found all this rather odd and exacting; but I was out to learn something of the world, and this was a part of it. On that occasion, for two or three days, I tried to do my duty; but duty in my ethics means a debt, an obligation freely undertaken; and I saw at once that I was unfit to live under a free government where other people voted as to what I should do. My unfitness must have transpired, for I was never asked again to Manchester-by-the-Sea, nor should I have been tempted. When later I knew how the other children of "Uncle Russell" lived in England, although, as I was informed, all had equal fortunes, this family seemed to belong to a different social class. Among the truly noble, as for instance in Spain, there was grandeur without much luxury or comfort; under the plutocracy, in which "Cousin Russell's" English brothers lived, there was luxury without grandeur; and in the bourgeoisie, which "Cousin Russell" himself had joined, there was comfort without luxury. Comfort, in his case, was stiffened by Spartan and athletic austerities, yet in sentimental directions he was soft enough. He was pleased with his appearance, being well built, portly, with fair side-whiskers that flew backward as he marched about; and of a summer evening he and his wife would stand embraced by the window, gazing alternately at each other and at the sunset over the sea. I knew this was a form of evening prayer, a wordless *Angelus*, and I stood discreetly aside.

At about the same time I made a first visit to another of "Uncle Russell's" children, "Cousin Lucy Codman" and her family, at their country house at Cotuit on Cape Cod. It was a much softer, sandier, flatter, poorer region than the Massachusetts "North Shore," with few summer residents, and little but scrub pine woods, straggling farms, and ghostly, gaunt natives who "made remarks." On the other hand the Codmans, in spite of their name so appropriate to Cape Cod, seemed almost to be living in England, with all the freedom, largeness, and tact of good society. You were taken for granted, put at your ease, made materially and morally comfortable. Conversation was spontaneous, unpretending, intelligent; you could talk about what interested you— if you did so with discretion and briefly; and you were not asked for your opinion on things you cared nothing about. The house was agreeably furnished, not over-furnished: there were flowers, a little music, enough wit to make express entertainments unnecessary. The father and the two elder sons were away—kept in Boston by their work; but the youngest son, Julian, sometimes took me out sailing in a cat-boat in very smooth water, a peaceful somnolent amusement very much to my taste. He was destined to become the most confidential of all my young friends in the following years, and I have already described him, his career, and the perfect sympathy there was between us. Julian, with the cat-boat, comes under the head of friendship, not of Boston society: and it was not on his account that I was invited to Cotuit.

I had been expressly summoned in order that I might make the acquaintance of Howard Sturgis, "Cousin Lucy's" youngest brother, who might well have been her son, being then thirty-three years of age. Howard, too, comes properly under the head of friendship, since I began the next year to make him almost yearly visits, sometimes reduplicated, at his house in Windsor: but since I first saw him in America, and it was my Sturgis connection that established a kind of family intimacy between us, I will say something about him here.

He had come to America for a complete change of scene, hoping it might help to heal the wound that, in his excessively tender heart, had been left by the death of his mother. She had not been, from all I have gathered, at all a remarkable woman, but luxurious and affectionate, surrounded in London by a few rich American friends, especially the daughters of Motley, the historian, who were married to Englishmen, and surrounded beyond them, more by hearsay than acquaintance, by the whole British aristocracy. Howard had been her last and permanent baby. The dear child was sensitive and affectionate, with abundant golden hair, large blue eyes, and well-turned chubby arms and legs. Her boudoir became his nursery and his playroom. As if by miracle, for he was wonderfully imitative, he became, save for the accident of sex, which was not yet a serious encumbrance, a perfect young lady of the Victorian type. He acquired a good accent in French, German and Italian, and instinctively embraced the proper liberal humanitarian principles in politics and history. There was an absolutely right and an absolutely wrong side in every war and every election; only the wicked, selfish, and heartless still prevented the deserving from growing rich, and maintained an absurd and cruel ascendency of birth, superstition, and military power. These were the sentiments of the Great Merchants, economists and reformers of the early nineteenth century, and Howard would have embraced them in any case because they appealed to his heart, and his feminine nature would never have allowed his intellect, no matter how keen, to do anything but defend his emotions. When women's opinions waver, it means that their hearts are not at rest. Let them once settle their affections and see their interests, and theoretical doubt becomes impossible for them. Howard's affections and interests were inextricably bound up with the liberal epoch; and no evidence would ever have convinced him that this was the only ground for his liberal dogmatism.

This was not all that he imbibed from his mother's circle. He was not only imitative, but he also had a theory that there was nothing women did that a man couldn't do better. Pride therefore seconded inclination in making him vie with the ladies and surpass them. He learned to sew, to embroider, to knit, and to do crochet; these occupations were not only guiltless of any country's blood, but helped to pass away the empty hours. He became wedded to them, and all his life, whether he sat by the fire or in his garden, his work-basket stood by his low chair. His needlework was exquisite, and he not only executed gorgeous embroideries, but designed them, for he was clever also with the pencil. Imitation, or a sort of involuntary caricature, sometimes went further with him. He would emit little frightened cries, if the cab he was in turned too fast round a corner; and in crossing a muddy road he would pick up the edge of his short covert-coat, as the ladies in those days picked up their trailing skirts.

Some of these automatisms were so extreme and so ridiculous that I can't help suspecting that there was something hypnotic or somnambulistic about them. He was too intelligent and too satirical to have done such things if he could have helped it. There may have been some early fixation at work, probably to his mother, of the kind that induces dreams, and develops into grotesque exaggerations and symbolic fancies. He mimicked people, sometimes on purpose, but often involuntarily: and his imagination penetrated their motives and thoughts, as his novels show, not necessarily with truth, but plausibly and with an endless capacity for extensions. He may have been at times the victim of this dramatic fertility in his own person, and found himself playing a part that the real circumstances did not call for.

He had not yet written his best novels, only an ultra-pathetic story about a little boy "Tim"; but one morning we found him sitting in the porch outside the living-room, on one of the wicker chairs with red-cotton cushions that adorned it, and that he copied later in the addition made to Queen's Acre; and we found him armed, not with his usual work-basket, but with a red leather writing case. He had an absorbed and far-away air. He was writing poetry: verses about the loss of his mother. We asked him to read them: he would not have brought them downstairs if he wished them to bloom and die unseen. He read them very nicely, without self-consciousness or affectation: the sentiment was intimate, but the form restrained and tactful.

Courage and distinction will save a man in almost any predicament; and Howard had been at Eton, where he acquired distinction and showed remarkable courage. Sending him there must have been a last desperate measure insisted on by his brothers, to cure him of his girlishness. A cruel remedy, it might seem, as if he had been sent to sea before the mast. Why hadn't his father and mother corrected him sooner? His father's mind had been growing feeble, and his mother probably thought the lad sweeter as he was. After all, too, they were Bostonians; and would it have been *right* to correct dear little sweet Howard for girlishness, when girlishness wasn't *morally wrong?* Let him go to Eton, properly safeguarded, if his brothers thought it absolutely necessary. And this heroic remedy didn't prove in the least cruel, or in the least efficacious. Young Howard calmly defied all those school-boys with his feminine habits and arts, which he never dreamt of disguising. He was protected by his wit and intellectual assurance; while his tutor, Mr. Ainger, author of the *Carmen Etonense,* and the two Misses Ainger, adopted him and screened him from the rude mob. Besides, Howard attracted affection, and however astonished one might be at first, or even scornful, one was always won over in the end.

After Eton, Trinity College, Cambridge was plain sailing, and confirmed his humanitarian principles and aristocratic habits. His studies don't seem to have been serious; but he remembered what he had read of belles-lettres, just as ladies do. He had even dipped into Berkeley's philosophy and had laid it aside, not unwisely, as an academic curiosity. To see interesting people, or at least fashionable people, and to hear about them, made his chief entertainment later. Of course he had travelled abroad and seen everything that everybody should see; he remained old-fashioned, without preraphaelite affectations, in matters of art. His novels were exquisitely felt and observed, full of delicately satirical phrases, and not without an obvious moral aimed against domestic prejudice and social tyranny: but his writing had hardly force enough, either in style or in thought, to leave a lasting impression.

In what he felt to be his homeless plight, he had looked about

for a house, and had finally taken a small one, with a nice garden
on the outskirts of Windsor Park. Its name had been Queensmead,
but there was a Kingsmead next door, and seeing that the land
was little more than an acre—at least the part of it visible from
the house—he re-christened it Queen's Acre, familiarly and ironically abbreviated to Quaker. The nearness of Eton, and of the
Aingers, had attracted him, for as often happens, he retained a
much greater affection for his school than for his College or University. In those first years his garden and his table were often
enlivened by groups of Eton boys. To some of them he gave pet
names, such as The Lion, The Bear, or The Babe; this last being
Willie Haines Smith, a distant cousin of his, who became his
adopted younger brother and companion for life.

All this lay in the future, and in England. For the moment at
Cotuit, although Howard was the guest of honour, the ruling
spirits were the ladies. There were two daughters, both in the
early twenties. Something, I hardly know what, seemed to desig-
nate the one in whom I ought to be particularly interested. I liked
them both; but to choose a wife was the last thing that I was
thinking of; my friends knew it, and this delicate question, never
spoken of, was left hanging in mid-air, until years later, when
one day Julian deliberately asked me why I didn't marry. I replied
that I wished to be free and didn't intend to live always in
America. Whether Julian's mother had prompted him to ask that
question, I don't know, perhaps not, since she had no reason to
desire me for a son-in-law, and her daughters, on approaching
the age of thirty, made reasonable and more suitable marriages.
Yet, out of sheer kindness, she seems to have taken an interest
in my happiness, as she conceived it ought to be; for she took
pains to go and tell my mother, whom she seldom visited, *how
strongly she felt* about certain things one of which was the *sad
mistake* that a poor young man made sometimes in backing away
from a rich girl, simply because she was rich, when they sincerely
cared for each other. This arrow was of course aimed at a particular target, but couldn't regard "Cousin Lucy's" daughters,

since they were not rich: so far from rich, indeed, that a poor young man couldn't have married them, no matter how often he had popped the question and been accepted. It would have meant a long engagement, with an eventual descent into another level of society.

I think I know what "Cousin Lucy" had in mind. She was spinning a romance out of a nascent sympathy between a certain distinguished heiress and me; it never went beyond agreeable conversations about books, operas, plays, and travels, merely at dinners and other social functions. Had I been in love with her, and pressed my suit, she might have made the mistake of accepting me, to the consternation of her numerous relations; but I didn't allow myself to fathom the question whether I was in love with her or not. The barrier was not her person nor the fact that she was rich; this fact was precisely what might have encouraged me, because I should not have been imposing any material sacrifices upon her; but she would have been imposing upon me her whole background, her country, her family, her houses, her religion. Not that I had any fault to find with these things *for her*; but a *déraciné,* a man who has been torn up by the roots, cannot be replanted and should never propagate his kind. In the matter of religion, for instance, I found myself in this blind alley. I was not a believer in what my religion, or any religion, teaches dogmatically; yet I wouldn't for the world have had a wife or children dead to religion. Had I lived always in Spain, even with my present philosophy, I should have found no difficulty: my family would have been Catholic like every other family; and the philosophy of religion, if ever eventually discussed among us, would have been a subsequent private speculation, with no direct social consequences. But living in a Protestant country, the free-thinking Catholic is in a socially impossible position. He cannot demand that his wife and children be Catholics, since he is not, in a controversial sense, a Catholic himself; yet he cannot bear that they should be Protestants or freethinkers, without any Catholic tradition or feelings. They would not then be his wife or children except by accident: they would not belong to his people. I know that there are some who accept this consequence, even pretend to have become Protestants, and bury as deep as possible the fact that they were born Catholics or Jews. But I am not a man of that stamp. I have been involuntarily uprooted. I accept the intellectual advantages of that position, with its social and moral disqualifications. And I refuse to be annexed, to be abolished, or to be grafted onto any plant of a different species.

This feeling was absolutely fixed in me from the beginning, but didn't prevent me from liking the Boston ladies, though I never courted any of them. I liked the elegance, the banter, the wit and intelligence that often appeared in them. I liked to sit next to them at dinner, when conversation flowed more easily and became more civilised in the midst of lights and flowers, good food and good wines. The charm of the ladies was a part of that luxurious scene, of that polite intoxication: for me it was nothing more. But people didn't understand that this could be all: even my sister Susana didn't understand it and more or less seriously looked about for someone with whom to pair me off. This was when we were children; later when I began to find my real affinities, Susana had returned to Spain, and perhaps had seen that I had not thought of marrying anyone in Boston, not even among the Catholics.

My real affinities were with three or four elderly ladies, who never appeared off the social stage, and who like me were more or less spontaneously playing a part, as it were, in public, while their real and much less interesting life lay hidden beneath, like the water-supply, the drains, and the foundations of their houses. They were all childless, or had lost their children, and their husbands, when living, either didn't appear at all in the same scenes, or played a subordinate, comic, errand-boy part in them. The invisible husband might be, in his own world, an important person, esteemed as much or more than his wife in hers: but like royal spouses occupying opposite wings in a palace, they had their own exits and entrances, their own hours and their own friends. This was the case with two leading ladies in the Boston of my time, Mrs. Gardner and Mrs. Whitman. Often as I lunched and visited at Mrs. Gardner's, both in town and country, I hardly ever saw her husband; and it was only after years of acquaintance with Mrs. Whitman that once, at a week-end party by the sea, I caught sight of Mr. Whitman: not that he was living in the house or belonged to the house-party, but that he had come, as if by chance, in his yacht, and had looked in upon us.

These two ladies had individual vocations; their husbands had their own position, their own work, and their own friends, and having ample separate means they amicably cultivated separate gardens. Mrs. Gardner was not a Bostonian: her vocation was to show Boston what it was missing. Instead of following the fashion, she undertook to set it. It wasn't followed; Boston doggedly stuck to its old ways and its old people: yet it couldn't ignore Mrs. Gardner; her husband was an old Bostonian and always countenanced, supported, and (invisibly) stood by her; and she had an indefatigable energy and perseverance that, in spite of all murmurs and hesitations, carried the day. When she became a widow and built her Venetian palace in The Fenway, as Egyptian monarchs built their tombs and went to live in them, she became an acknowledged public benefactor. Criticism was hushed: and there was something moving in beholding this old lady, whose pleasure it had been to shock, devoting herself more and more modestly to preparing and completing her museum, to be left to the town that she had startled when younger, that had long looked at her askance, and that she was now endowing with all her treasures.

What her inner life may have been, her religion (she was outwardly a very High Church Anglican) or her sentiments regarding Boston, her husband, or the child she had lost, and regarding the works of art and the artists that she devoted herself to collecting, I do not know: but it is easy to perceive the figure that she wished to cut in the world. She modelled herself on the great ladies of French and Italian society, as she had seen them in her travels or during her residence in Venice. She was far from beautiful, but she knew that this was no obstacle to dressing magnificently and boldly, or being positively alluring: her clothes (for the evening) filled Boston with alarm and with envy. She was not of good family, although professedly related to the royal house of Stuart; but she gave Boston a lesson in being aristocratic, and surrounded herself with interesting people, strangers, artists, musicians, and anyone who was either distinguished or agreeable. If the old Bostonians didn't like it, they needn't come; but they came, if they were asked.

She followed the fashion of the 1890's in collecting real or alleged works of the Old Masters, and also of some modern painters; but here the state of society in the twentieth century and in America prevented her from collecting as an aristocrat might, for his own pleasure, to enhance the surroundings of his life and the heritage of his family. She collected to collect; and such collections can have only one end, a public museum. This fatality, imposed by circumstances, worked a slow and subtle change in her bearing and in her satisfactions. She became an agent for her own museum. At least, so she seemed in her public capicity, for by building her museum she became a public character: but her personality never was quite transformed. I may say that I have never really seen her collection; for she would insist on showing me everything, instead of letting me—as a true *grande dame* might have done—ramble about without her and study what caught my eye; and when she showed her treasures, she would tell something about them, where she found them, or their history, and there would always be the personal play of conversation between her and her guest: so that the guest had a charming half-hour with her, but never *saw* any of her things. I should have bought a ticket and gone to her museum on the days when it was open to the public; but I dislike museums and never did so, especially as I heard that sometimes she walked about even on public days and acted as cicerone. Her palace and her pictures had become the last costume and the last audacity by which she would vanquish old Boston.

Mrs. Gardner, though she defied prudery, practised the virtue most difficult for a brilliant woman in a hostile society: she spoke ill of nobody. She joined kindness to liberty; and she played the queen and the connoisseur with so much good nature that in her masquerade she was aware of no rival, while in the real world she scattered substantial favours.

More in the spirit of Boston, more conscientious and troubled, was Mrs. Whitman. Not content merely to love the fine arts, she became an artist and designed stained-glass windows. There were echoes in her of Transcendentalism, but no longer imageless nor countrified. It had become symbolic, ritualistic, luxurious. I remember the high wax candles, as on an altar, decorating her dinner table. She didn't make a point of entertaining itinerant artists or other celebrities; but devoted herself to instilling the higher spirit of the arts and crafts into the minds of working-girls. Our good works, alas, are often vainer than our vanities. "What did Mrs. Whitman talk to you about?" somebody asked after a lecture. And one of the girls replied: "She said that art was green." It is true that Mrs. Whitman was partial to that colour, and Mahomet expressed the same preference, for an easily assignable reason: but when we express preferences, though we may diffuse those preferences by mere suggestion or hypnosis, we incite others to express their contrary preferences, and to nurse every preference, instinctive or imposed, out of pure doggedness.

This is not an incitement to learn, but to be content without learning: the great temptation of freedom. Mrs. Whitman's lecture, in the case of that working-girl, was a complete failure. If she had reported the *explicable* fact that Mahomet thought green the most beautiful of colours, something might have been gained; because the working-girl's casual preference for pink or for blue would have been not merely challenged but undermined. For if Mahomet loved green, because he constantly travelled through deserts, looking for the palm trees of some oasis, what desert are you, poor working-girl, travelling through, that causes you to long for pink and blue ribbons? If you reflect upon that, the apparently inane conclusion that art is green might acquire a pregnant meaning. Art would appeal to the mind in general as the colour green appealed to the eye of Mahomet, and for similar reasons. We must consider human nature and the radical predicaments of the living arts if we are to recover definite taste or artistic power. The aestheticism of the nineteenth century was a symptom of decay, aggravated by the pathos of distance.

Mrs. Whitman was a great friend of William James. They had similar impetuous perceptions and emotions, a similar unrest, and a similar desire to penetrate to the hidden facts, the submerged classes, the neglected ideas, unpleasing to the official world. The generosity of all this was evident: less evident was the fruitfulness of it. The field was vague and so was the mind of the reformers. One day James asked me to come to a supper that he was giving for his more advanced pupils, about thirty of them. Mrs. Whitman was coming. He wished me to come too—without dressing, of course—and help Mrs. Whitman to feel at home. And I was placed at her right hand, James sitting opposite, in the middle of the other long side of the table. Neither Mrs. James nor any other member of the family was present: it was to be a philosophical conclave, a semi-religious semi-festive mystery. Why did James conceive such a supper? Out of kindness, to be hospitable and fatherly towards his disciples. But why did he ask Mrs. Whitman, or why did she wish to come? Mrs. James could have been equally hospitable and kind. Perhaps it was not from the young men's point of view, but from Mrs. Whitman's, that he saw the desirability of inviting her. She was interested in diffusing high aspirations among the people: here she would see a chosen group of ambitious young men, and perhaps scatter some good seed or get some hint or some encouragement in her work. The young men were of course impressed, some of them no doubt dazzled, by James in his own library, walled completely with books, save for his father's portrait in oils over the mantelpiece, and by the lordly supper—with a touch of the *Kneipe* about it, for we all had beer, except Mrs. Whitman. For her a half-bottle of champagne was provided, which, as James said, would not be good for the rest of us. Above all they must have retained a striking image of Mrs. Whitman, beautifully dressed, not in an evening gown, but in a green velvet bodice with long sleeves, delicately set off by gold braid, an ample white silk skirt, and a large bunch of violets. She was not particularly beautiful, nor the opposite (as Mrs. Gardner was) but she had that vivacity and intelligence, added to the discreet arts of the toilet, that keep French ladies from ever looking old. I doubt that she said anything that any of those young men would note or remember. I had been summoned expressly to entertain her, and spare her the effort of having to make talk with shy uncouth youths all the evening; for there were no speeches. In philanthropic and propagandist directions I doubt that anything was accomplished: but the feast was rather beautiful in itself, and certainly cannot have been forgotten by any of those who were there. It was an instance of the manner in which those two distinguished spirits, William James and Mrs. Whitman, failed to diffuse their intended influence, and yet succeeded while failing: for they added something pleasant and pure to the world.

As to the male element in Boston society, it would perhaps be better for me not to say anything. I knew few of them well, because most of my friends, even at Harvard, were not Bostonians, and those who were Bostonians were seldom seen at parties. The men went there to see the women, and were like fish out of water in regard to one another. Besides, Boston society was dominated by the very young, except in staid elderly circles that met only at dinners. Sometimes, being a conveniently unattached bachelor, I was honoured by an invitation to small parties of that sort, at houses where I was not intimate. On such occasions I might make the acquaintance of representative elderly men, or hear them talk, when conversation became general. One distinguished Bostonian that I came to know in this way was Judge Holmes. His wife never went anywhere, and he, still rather youngish with a sweeping blond moustache, would play the bachelor. One day—

this was at Mrs. Gray's, who had been a Boston "beauty"—he said he didn't like to walk in Beacon Street. Every door seemed to him the tombstone of a dead love. This was one direction in which the Justice unbent; but his mind was plastic also in speculation. Being an exceptionally successful man he could be pessimistic in philosophy, and being an old Bostonian he could disinterestedly advocate democratic reforms. After I had left America he surprised me by writing in high terms about my *Winds of Doctrine*, especially the first page in which there is nothing not commonplace except perhaps the tone in which moral and political revolutions are spoken of, as natural episodes in a transformation without end. It is or it was usual, especially in America, to regard the polity of which you happen to approve as sure to be presently established everywhere and to prevail forever after. To have escaped this moralistic obsession, at least for a moment, evidently was a pleasure to Judge Holmes. He had a really liberal, I mean a truly free, mind.

There was another local celebrity whom I once heard discourse about politics at a dinner, not in a set speech, but in ordinary conversation. Everybody else stopped talking in order to listen to him because, by a rare exception in his class, he had gone into politics and been Governor of Massachusetts. His name was Roger Wolcott, and in his young days he had been regarded as the handsomest man and the greatest beau in Boston. He was attacking the New York *Nation*, a weekly paper which I always read. Its politics were radical, but the book reviews were written by professors, often professors of foreign languages, about subjects that interested me. The views of the professorial class, or intelligentsia, are naturally literary and captious; Roger Wolcott, as a man and as a practical politician, detested them. He said *The Nation* had a very bad influence in the country, especially among the young men. It gave them a false idea of what government was and ought to be. It made them ignorantly critical, supercilious, unpatriotic. As far as I remember, Wolcott didn't go beyond bare denunciation; he was probably not speculative, like Judge Holmes;

and he might seem to have been guided merely by club spirit or esprit de corps like so many Lodges and Greek Letter Fraternities that flourished in America without representing any genuine public interests. On the other hand, his experience may have given him some true intuition of the fated movement and destiny of his country, and his "stalwart" politics may have been only a vulgar cover for something heroic: I mean, for the courage and pride of sharing the life of his country, in soul as well as in body.

CHAPTER VII

AMERICANS IN EUROPE

MORE than with any other class of people, fate has associated me with Americans in Europe. Even when I was still living in the United States, it was people at home in Europe, socially and morally, that most readily became my friends. Not that being at home in Europe or at home in America counted in itself in my true friendships. That which counted in that case was exclusively the individual man or woman, the body and the soul. A field of action and of thought was essential, but only as a language is essential for conveying a thought: for when the thought is absorbing, the language is not noticed, and seems indifferent. Yet a common language, a common social and moral idiom, becomes in itself a great bond when you are travelling in strange places, among people with whom you cannot communicate. The common language draws you together, even if what each will say may eventually not prove important or acceptable to the others.

Now with Americans in Europe I had a common field of experience, a common social and moral convention, and we were for the moment in the same boat. A travelling acquaintance may of course disclose a vital affinity: but I think this was not the case with any of my American friends in Europe: either no vital affinity existed or we had discovered it in America, and it was independent of all accidents of residence. With converts of any kind, with American women married to Englishmen, with expatriates, with aesthetic souls that fled from America because the voices there were too rough, I never had much sympathy. It was persons who were thoroughly European or thoroughly American that held the first place in my esteem. In my esteem, but not in my life. In my life the foreground was filled with Americans in Europe.

This appears emphatically in the case of Strong, the only person not of my kindred with whom I have lived, on and off, for years. I have described the origin of our friendship and its not altogether satisfactory result. Why did Strong live in Europe at all? It would require more knowledge than our life-long acquaintance has given me to answer this question properly: there are mysteries involved, and Strong was more than reserved, he was inhibited, in regard to his private affairs. I can only point to the gross facts: he had been at school in Germany; he very naturally wished to return to Germany to study philosophy; and, then, when from Germany we had gone to London for our holidays, in the spring of 1887, he one day announced that *it would be best* for him to leave me and go to Paris to join his father, who was there with a party of friends. This sounded dutiful and pious enough; it was not for me to ask any questions, nor did I suspect any mystery. But a month or two later, I received a letter, saying that he had been travelling with Mr. John D. Rockefeller and family, and that he was engaged to be married to the eldest daughter, Bessie; that they were all coming to England in June; and that Mr. Rockefeller invited me to join them, on the day of Queen Victoria's Jubilee, to view the procession from a room he had engaged in Buckingham Palace Road. Not a word more. Had the pious rogue been engaged all the time to this fabulously rich heiress, when he generously consented to divide the Walker Fellowship with me? I can hardly think so. It must all have been a machination behind his back. His father and Mr. Rockefeller, eminent Baptist elders, had thought *it would be best* to settle these young people safely and happily for life, before they got any foolish notions into their heads. Old Dr. Strong (who was himself becoming a financier, had a red nose, and liked good dinners with plenty of champagne) saw a brilliant future assured for his son; and this marriage would rivet Rockefeller even more tightly to himself and to all the Baptist institutions; while Rockefeller saw his daughter, his favourite child, whose future gave him some anxiety, safely settled with a good-looking, high-principled young man sure to make her happy, and with his studious habits and mild disposition never to separate her from her father, either in place of residence or in sound Christian sentiments. The young people were willing enough. Both were probably profoundly bored and with a blank future. To be married was a new idea. It gave them something almost exciting to think about and to do.

In his old age Strong sometimes amused himself by writing "poetry." The most interesting of these effusions recounts how he loved five times, and Bessie, his wife, is one of these lady-loves, but evidently not the one secretly preferred. From this and from other indications I gather that he *thought it would be best,* after having been obliged by his conscience to resist the higher Baptist powers in regard to his religious allegiance, not to resist them in this, that seemed a reasonable proposal. People would think it a piece of incredible good fortune, but somehow for him it was sad.

In Buckingham Palace Road, on the appointed day, I was duly introduced to the great millionaire, still a dapper, youngish man with cordial American manners, and to his daughter Bessie, not at all the blushing bride, but the image of vigorous health and good sense, nice-looking, frank, and with manlike college airs, for she was fresh from Vassar. Our conversation corresponded, and was nothing but commonplaces helped out by smiles. Little did I suspect that I should never have a chance to talk with her rationally again; for even when I stayed in later years at her house, I hardly ever saw her. She was always, as they put it, in delicate health, which was a euphemism for not being in her right mind. It was to be Strong's destiny to become a sort of guardian or watchman over his invalid wife. At Compiègne, during her last years, he would see her for ten minutes in the morning, and for ten minutes again in the evening, each time bringing her a picture post-card to talk about. He had a great collection of them in stock, and dealt them out, as if just discovered, two each day, for her to put in her album.

Ten years later, when I was at King's College, the Rockefellers invited me again to see the Queen's procession, when she drove to the service in front of St. Paul's in thanksgiving for her sixty years' reign. This time we were in a room in Piccadilly; and the sight so absorbed me, with its vast historic and political suggestions, that I don't remember Rockefeller being there at all or any of the other guests. On another occasion, however, when I went to spend a holiday with Strong at Lakewood, New Jersey, I had a capital opportunity of learning some of the great capitalist's characteristics; for the house was his, he had only lent it to his daughter and son-in-law, and at that time he was living in it, in order to be near his private golf-links, where his own larger house had been closed for the winter. I saw him only at table; but as Strong was a silent man, and his wife was ill upstairs, it was practically with me that Mr. Rockefeller had to talk. He played golf assiduously, always alone, matching his score on one day against his score on another; just what the saints do when they daily examine their conscience and consider whether they have developed any new sins, or been carried by the grace of God one step forward towards perfection. Such was probably also the interest dominating Rockefeller's chase after millions. He was beyond comparing himself with his competitors; he compared himself with himself.

One day when I had mentioned Spain, he asked me, after a little pause, what was the population of Spain. I said I believed it was then nineteen millions. There was another pause, this time rather longer, and then he said, half to himself: "I must tell them at the office that they don't sell enough oil in Spain. They must look the matter up."

I saw in my mind's eye the ideal of the monopolist. All nations must consume the same things, in proportion to their population. All mankind will then form a perfect democracy, supplied with rations from a single centre of administration, as is for their benefit; since they will then secure everything assigned to them at the lowest possible price. This was not a subject for me to broach with Rockefeller; but I ventured a hint in another direction, which I don't know whether he caught. In Avila, for I couldn't speak for the whole of Spain, we had passed from olive oil and candles almost directly to electricity. Gas we had never known, but petroleum had been used in cafés and shops, and perhaps in one room in each house, in a lamp over the centre table, under which burned the charcoal *brasero;* but even in Avila the electric bulb was beginning to supersede it. The world changed rapidly, when we once set it changing. Yet the Standard Oil Company had no cause for alarm. Motors were coming in, and petrol would be more in demand than ever.

Another day, in the act of sitting down at table, as if he had something important on his mind, Mr. Rockefeller formally addressed his son-in-law. "Charles, I heard that you had been buying a cord of wood, and I went down to the cellar to look at it. *That* isn't a cord of wood. When I was a young fellow I used to cut a cord of wood, and I know what it looks like. I don't need a tape-measure to measure it with. They are cheating you."

Poor Strong said nothing, and I, trying to be sympathetic, observed that sometimes, when values changed, dealers found it simpler to reduce the measure than to raise the price. As a baker's dozen is more than twelve, so a conventional cord of wood to-day at Lakewood might be less than a natural cord of wood in Mr. Rockefeller's boyhood. Besides, things come to seem smaller as we grow bigger; and wasn't it possible that a part of the wood might have been burned already? My wisdom, however, seemed to fall flat and we talked of something else.

Rockefeller himself had changed surprisingly to the eye. From looking much younger than he must have been in 1887, he now looked immeasurably old. He had lost all hair, eyebrows and eyelashes included, and wore a pepper and salt wig decidedly too small for him. His skin, too, was curiously wrinkled, and he was elaborately wrapped up for his long day on the golf-links. But I understood that he remained the active head of his Company, and had a private wire to his office for receiving information and giving orders.

Strong's marriage had been arranged in France, and after it, it was in France that he and his wife lingered. They learned French conscientiously, and to become perfectly fluent, they agreed always to speak French together at table. This habit grew upon Mrs. Strong, until she refused to speak English at all; and when I last saw her, both she and Margaret, then about ten years old, had French nurses and would speak nothing but French. This habit, and the habit of constantly returning to France, had not been adopted deliberately. Strong was as firmly convinced of the wisdom and duty of living in his own country as were his family and the Rockefellers: but the state of his wife's health and spirits seemed to demand a frequent season abroad, and later his own health and spirits seemed to demand it also. He had not given up his intended profession, and for one year was instructor in psychology at Cornell. Here his wife's health again interfered, and that position was given up. They would live at Lakewood, and he would become an associate professor—this could be easily arranged by Mr. Rockefeller—at Columbia. Nevertheless, they were almost always in France; and Strong became attached to a limited but well-chosen group of resorts, to which he introduced me: Versailles, Saint-Germain, Fontainebleau, Compiègne, Aix-les-Bains, and Glion in French Switzerland. To two of these, the first and the last, I often returned alone in later years, finding them quiet and inspiring.

After his wife's death, Strong made a heroic effort to settle down in New York. He took a flat in an apartment house with a general restaurant, on Fifth Avenue, and a governess for Margaret; and he undertook his proposed teaching at Columbia. In his eagerness to begin work, he arrived on the first morning rather early at his lecture room. As yet there was no one there. He would have a moment to rest, and to look over his notes, recalling the chief points to be made in due order, before the students began to come in. When he looked at his watch again, the appointed hour had arrived, but still no students. It was customary to allow five or ten minutes for them to straggle from one lecture room to another. Five minutes, ten minutes passed, and not a soul. Was nobody taking his course at all? He must not be precipitate. There might have been some mistake about the room. He would wait another five minutes. At a quarter past the hour, he resolutely gathered up his papers, put on his coat and hat, and thought of the Apostles bidden to shake the dust from their feet. But resentment and mortification, if he felt them, were soon buried deep among forgotten dreams. The feeling that rose to the surface was one of relief. He made his way to the College Office. There he explained to the clerk that he was Professor Strong. Could they inform him if anybody had elected his special course in psychology? They would see. They had a list of all elective courses, with the number of students that had chosen each. No: there was no tally against that special course in psychology. Perhaps it was rather a graduate course. They would let him know if there were inquiries about it.

On his way home the feeling of relief gained upon Strong. He had done his duty. His important but neglected theory of perception, more accurate and scientific than any other, could be better explained in a book than in lectures to beginners. Now he could devote the winter to that necessary task. For the sake of his work, he must be careful about his health. His mind always worked better in a mild climate. He would stop at the up-town office of the Italian Steamship Company and engage cabins on their first boat for Naples. That old convent above the road to Amalfi would be a place to suit him perfectly: quiet, sunny, simple and healthy.

Italian food and habits, however, proved less favourable for work than he had hoped. The demon that pursued Strong everywhere was *ennui*. In Paris, at least, he could, as he put it, "attend the Comédie Française"; and every day he could sit for an hour or two in front of a café, *la Régence, les Deux Magots,* or *la Closerie des Lilas.* That made a little change of scene; and sometimes American acquaintances would come and speak to him. Finally he took an apartment on the third floor at Number 9, Avenue de l'Observatoire. The place was clean and quiet, no passing, and nothing but sky and a wall of trees visible from the windows. The *salon* had been decorated in the style of Louis Seize, with silk panels, but Strong ordered the silk to be removed and the panels painted a dull white, to match the mouldings; and he "purchased" English furniture at Maples', of the sort usually covered with gay chintz, to which he was not accustomed. He had it covered instead with a strong reddish-gray stuff to match the curtains; and a great walnut bookcase was made to run along one whole wall. The room was brilliantly lighted by three large windows, yet somehow seemed sad and unfinished. Strong hadn't the secret of making himself comfortable, and here, as at Fiesole later, he was always thinking of going somewhere else for a change.

To tell his whole tragic history, and that of his daughter, would require volumes, with profound knowledge of families and circles that I have never frequented. It would carry me too far from the persons and places that have left vivid images in my mind. I therefore bequeath the subject to any novelist that it might tempt; for it would be a great subject. As a mere hint, however, of the perspectives to be disclosed I will describe a single episode that I happen to have witnessed.

Strong, and even more his daughter Margaret, were condemned to move within the magnetic field of the Rockefeller millions. Not a few roving atoms, positively electrified, circled and buzzed within it. Among Margaret's Parisian friends were the Marquise de Blanc-Blanc and her daughter. The Marquise had little money and only one son, already the Marquis and as yet unmarried. One day we had word that she was coming to see Monsieur Strong— he was laid up with paralysis of the legs—for an important consultation. Her daughter accompanied her, but at once carried Margaret off to some concert or to some dressmaker's, so as to leave the elderly people unembarrassed in discussing business.

Strong had expressly asked me to remain. When tea had been served, Madame de Blanc-Blanc, with a perceptible air of addressing the public, began to speak of her son. "We have," she said, "the most satisfactory reports of his work in Poland. You know, Messieurs, how much the government appreciated his services during the war. He is a young officer of intrepid character, with a quick temper and an iron will. He was invited to accept a very difficult, a very delicate post, the command of a company of criminals. His success with them was extraordinary. They became like sheep under him in camp, and like wolves in the battlefield. Men's energies, he thinks, should never be suppressed, no matter how violent. They must be turned into the right path. *Voilà tout!* What a lesson for his future wife, if she could only learn it! Now in Poland he has a task no less difficult, and he is meeting with equal success. Not criminals now, cadets. Cadets who have imbibed, under evil influences, wild notions of liberty. What is liberty? It is the right to do wrong whenever you choose. Yet my son inspires them with respect. He shows them the invincible order that God has established in the world. They learn to obey. They learn to command. Ah, he is a disciplinarian! Yet this severity in him goes with the tenderest heart, when once his heart has been touched. I, his mother, can assure you of it. He has been a good son. And they say a good son always makes a good husband."

Here Madame de Blanc-Blanc paused, sipped her cup of tea, nibbled the edge of a small cake, liked it, gobbled the rest of it, drank more tea, and proceeded.

"I regret that my son should have been called away before he could pay his respects to you, Monsieur, and to our dear Margaret. He knows through us how pretty, how simple, how charming, how exquisite and how appealing she is. A man of bold spirit and high temper, a man of action, especially loves gentleness and sweetness in women, and I think that a young girl like Margaret could not help admiring his soldierly qualities. Her tastes are as yet a little vague, and in the firmness of his character she would be relieved to find the natural solution to her indecision."

Here again the Marquise made a short pause, and then turned to me with evident premeditation.

"You, Monsieur," she said in a conciliatory tone, seeing that Strong hadn't at all melted, "being Spanish, must be a Catholic?"

"Yes, Madame, we are all still Catholics in Spain, at least nominally. But you know the character of this epoch. Most of us have lost our faith."

"Ah, I know it well. That is an effect of men's vices. It wears off. You will return to us some day." And glancing at me to estimate my age, she added, smiling, "You will return soon." Then, addressing Strong again, she went on.

"Ah, faith is so important! Without the faith, the family has no stability, no union, no security. No one recognises any obligation. Everyone is divorced. When public morality is so relaxed, there remains no law except within the Church. We must all be faithful children of the Church. Without that safeguard, no prudent man can venture to found a family."

At this point the bell rang. The young ladies returned from their outing, and almost immediately Madame de Blanc-Blanc and her daughter took their leave. No distinct proposal had been made. The lady hadn't come to ask for Margaret's hand, as we had expected. She had come to lay down a prior condition, namely, that Margaret should become a Catholic. This was not altogether a gratuitous suggestion. Margaret, when she had a Catholic governess, had shown a marked inclination to the Church, and still felt no hostility to it, only an incorrigible vagueness about everything. The whole affair lapsed; and it was well. Her proposed family, as I discovered by accident, were already making merciless fun of her behind her back.

I have mentioned that Bob Potter, when in the summer of 1892 I stayed with his family at Bar Harbor, was preoccupied with a love affair and with his approaching departure for Paris, to study at the Beaux-Arts. A little more than a year later, after the death of Warwick, both matters were happily settled, and I went to New York for his wedding. The bride's father, Mr. Nicholas Fish, had been for years American Minister at Brussels, and there his only daughter had been educated, learning to speak French and German perfectly. With these accomplishments, with the outlook that a diplomatic circle always opens out, and with her own quick intelligence, she had become an unusually charming person; and her ambitious parents expected that she should make a brilliant match. But she fell in love with Bob Potter, quite intelligibly, for he too was unusually *distingué* for a young New Yorker; but alas the Fishes thought him penniless: he had only just money enough to smoke good cigarettes. This, to the young lady's romantic mind, seemed quite enough for their conjoint happiness, and she threatened to run away with her lover to Paris, if they refused to consent to her marriage. The matter was compromised by arranging for a quiet wedding in the house with no promise of an allowance from the Fishes for the future.

During the next few years, I saw the Bob Potters but rarely in Paris, as I could be there only in transit; but these interviews sufficed to show me that, in this case, the marriage of a friend, far from being an obstacle to further good-fellowship, was an aid to it, because Mrs. Potter proved to be as good a friend as her husband. In 1897 we arranged to make a trip to Italy together; and Mrs. Potter secretly took Italian lessons, so as to be able to rescue us helpless men in all our linguistic difficulties. I had been in Italy two years earlier with Loeser; and this second journey with the Potters, partly over the same ground, showed me how important the human element is in our supposedly abstract interests. I saw Venice and Rome, and the pictures everywhere, in a new light. Bob was a professional architect, with French training: he was dazzled by the picturesque and somewhat religiously moved by the primitives; that was his Anglo-Saxon side; but he was shocked by the false façades of the baroque churches; they were stage settings, allowed to exhibit their shabby side. Yet in persons, as I would tell him, he appre-

ciated the charm and dignity of clothes, which were all *façades*
and *postiches*. Why shouldn't buildings, with their meagre material framework, expand also into decorative cloaks, ruffs, and
panaches? There was a kind of homage to the eye and to the ideal
in such a seemly masquerade. It presented what it would fain
be, and what it thought worthy of your attention. To seem less
grand would have been less courteous.

Bob taught me less about the arts than Loeser did; his knowledge was more limited. It was exclusively American and French.
But he taught me a great deal in matters of taste, because as
appeals to taste, as charming images, he appreciated all sorts of
perfection. The only difficulty here was the resulting sense of
frivolity and anarchy. The world became a carnival of butterflies.
Insight didn't penetrate to the organic, moral and physical energies that were expressed in each type of perfection, and that determined its rank and dignity in the real world. To have insisted
on this vital background, however, would have destroyed the
purity of taste, in its aristocratic independence; and there is a
subjective root to immediate pleasure in form and harmony just
as profound as the roots of the arts in the public world; more
profound, even, because the public world itself takes shape only in
obedience to the private capacities of the people that compose it.
The appeal, in a liberal mind, must ultimately be to pure taste, to
instinctive preference: and when Bob Potter, so very tall and thin,
so refined and so embarrassed, said *pfui!* or when he was religiously silent and evidently moved in the presence of something
exquisite, my own load was lifted, and I saw how instrumental
were all the labour and history of man, to be crowned, if crowned
at all, only in intuition.

In 1896–1897, when I was at King's College, some Harvard
friends studying at the Beaux Arts asked me to spend the Christmas
holidays with them in Paris, at No. 3, Rue Soufflot. They could
offer me a room, and I might contribute my share to the common
cost of their table. It was a pleasant way of seeing something, and
hearing more, of student life in the Quartier Latin; and topo-

graphically and linguistically, it helped to make me feel at home when I went later to live there with Strong.

The young men at the Rue Soufflot were only club acquaintances; later I had a real friend, Lawrence Butler, also at the Beaux-Arts, whom I often saw and visited, before and after, in America, although always, as it were, in the character of an American in Europe. It was in mid-ocean, in June 1895, that I made his acquaintance, when he was perhaps nineteen years old. I heard that he had fallen down the steep and curving stairs that led below to the cabin and had sprained his ankle. When two or three days later, I crossed him in that very place, I spoke to him. He was getting on, he said, and could move about with a crutch. This was the beginning of a very long and very satisfactory friendship. He was a well-bred youth and always kept his place as a *young* friend even when no longer very young: and this discretion on his part turned the difference in our ages from a difficulty into a pleasure. He asked me to stay at his house, and introduced me to his family, especially to his mother and to his favourite aunt, wife of Stanford White, the architect. He became an architect himself, though somewhat casually as to the practice of his profession, and this was a double bond, because his knowledge fell in with my tastes and his leisure with my habits.

His interest in building was human, domestic, proprietary: he was always thinking of *living* in his houses and *praying* in his churches. For beneath the surface, which was a sort of helpless herd-instinct, there was natural piety in him. He was affectionate and he was religious. I could be happy in his company. I used to tell him, and he agreed, that he ought to have been an English country gentleman. In Long Island, where he lived and where his mother's family had a sort of estate (since Smithtown and Garden City had been originally their land) things were too changeful and urbanised. There was no room for a landlord: there was only a land company. Nevertheless he had an ample house in the midst of woods far from all others, and even a toy cathedral in Garden City, which he looked after with special care. And his somewhat inarticulate inner man had another outlet. He sang very well: at least, he had a good tenor voice that promised great things, and that he took pains to cultivate, as he took pains to study architecture. In Paris Jean de Reszke gave him lessons, telling him to sing out and to shout—which was exactly what he could have done well and heartily. But like my luckless hero—Oliver Alden, to whom he contributed this trait—he could sing only what he felt.

Falling short, which was almost universal among those of my friends that had artistic or intellectual pretensions, was not always due to the materialism of the age, or to other untoward circumstances; not always even to being smothered in circumstances ironically too favourable. The cause seemed sometimes to be innate: dreaminess or somnambulism in a soul too vegetative to resist transformation or to transform anything else into its own image. Is it the fog of the North? That is what Nordics seem to think when they flock to the South for inspiration. They are then initiated into southern sensuality, as if into a warmer mysticism; but that doesn't enable them to accomplish anything definite. Is it immaturity? Perhaps we might say so, in a complimentary sense. Externally, in action and learning, they may be more than competent, they may be Titanic; yet there may remain undeveloped resources and potentialities within them; so that they feel always unsatisfied, reject all finalities, and elude all discipline.

The most Nordic of my American friends was so Nordic that he seemed an American only by accident. When he went home, everything seemed to him unnecessary and inhuman; and he was content to live in Paris among poor artists and working people, with none of the comforts or social pleasures among which he had been bred. His father, Dr. Slade, was a well-known Boston physician; but his mother was a Fräulein Hensler; and whatever Scandinavian tallness, blondness, calmness, vagueness, and migratory instinct may have been latent in her must have been concentrated in her son Conrad. He was very good-looking in the expressionless, statuesque manner, rowed with the 'varsity crew and allowed himself to do as others did around him; but inwardly he was extraordinarily solitary and independent, as if he still lived among the fiords. He had warm poetic passions, very un-American; no scruples, no tipsy gregarious impulse about indulging them, and no ribaldry. It all seemed to him a wonderful work of nature, like the revolution of the stars; and leading afterwards what in Boston would have passed for a most irregular life, he preserved an air of perfect purity and serenity, his blue eyes as clear and his thoughts as speculative as ever.

For some instinctive reason that I won't attempt to fathom, he became attached to me, and told me his love-affairs, which were, as poetry should be, simple, sensuous, and short. He didn't move at all in Boston society. His lady-loves were mature prima-donnas, or country lasses, or city waifs. In Paris, where he went at once in the hope of becoming a sculptor, he grew comparatively domestic and monogamous, following the ancient dictates of nature. He wandered, when the spirit moved, through Italy and Greece, and southern France, always with the eye of an artist and a prophet, seeking to divine the secret of the beautiful. In time he became a devout admirer of Renoir, who he said was the greatest painter since Rubens: for he himself had dabbled in painting more than in sculpture, without visible results in either, but with much subjective deepening of sentiment and perception. He could never explain to me in words what was the merit of Renoir and the other moderns; the merits I could discern in them were evidently not to the point. About Greek art he did give me a hint, that my knowledge is too superficial for me to follow out or to test. It concerned the priority of the skeleton and the movement in figures: the visible detail, even the visible outline, was to *grow* out of the attitude, not merely to catch it, as in a modern caricature. In that sense, he made some designs in silver-point after Greek coins, which seemed to me truly classic in spirit. It is the dynamic symbol to the mind, conveyed by means as simple as possible, that works the miracle: as to the detail of the image, the eye itself is inattentive, and the artist wastes his science.

In later years Slade was an impressive figure, tall, calm, stately, bald, with a great curly yellow beard with grey hairs in it; he looked like Leonardo da Vinci. The only change in his mind was a new, natural, and fixed affection. He had a little boy, and was wrapped up in the child. Then step-motherly nature smote him in his tender spot. The boy developed a disease of the bones; the doctors said it might be cured. I was never told of the end, and heard only of the child being wheeled about in his bed from one sunny beach to another, in the hope that the rays of the sun might penetrate to his crumbling bones, and heal him.

Another American expatriate of marked personality, though not an expatriate in Europe, differed from most of my friends in being a Westerner, in having read my books, and in our acquaintance having been cemented not so much in youth as in mature years. Andrew Green had been my pupil in College, and I had once asked him, seeing how good he was at field sports, why he didn't go in for football or running. He replied that he cared nothing for sport of any kind, and only did his high jump and his broad jump for a private reason. Not then, but years later, he told me what that reason had been. He liked to belong to the athletic squad because at the training table he could see a particular friend of his every day, whereas otherwise they would never come across each other. This was because the friend was a leader in the College world and Green an outsider. I knew what that meant in College; and the interesting thing was Green's supreme contempt for such barriers and his deliberate way of surmounting them when he thought it worth while.

His self-reliance and clear will continued to show themselves later. He went into business in Chicago expressly to make money quickly and to escape from business, exactly as I went into teaching, but more successfully; for in a few years he had made his little pile, went alone to China, and hired a junk to live in, while he sailed leisurely up and down the great rivers and explored the wonders of that country. Moral contrasts, moral liberty: aesthetic contrasts, aesthetic potentiality *ad infinitum*. No wonder that he read my books and understood them! Yet that was only the critical side of my philosophy, which people in my day could appreciate, even if they didn't trust it. That which escaped them, and probably escaped Green, was the deeper presupposition, without which all criticism would be futile: the need of singleness of mind and complete loyalty to the particular virtue possible to each age and to each individual.

What monstrous selfishness, I hear the Bostonians saying, to drop your work, never to think of the needs of others, and to run away and hide and lead an empty life of idleness at the antipodes! Yes, Green and I were unmitigated egoists: we thought before acting. We asked what the needs of others really were, and whether we were doing them any good. Had we been conscious of doing great good, as the Bostonians were, that feeling would have filled us with reflected happiness and zeal, and we should have gone on doing it. But were business men in Chicago or professors of philosophy at Harvard working for the good of others? Weren't they working to earn money or to propagate their views? Weren't they invading the public aggressively, with their enterprise or their propaganda, to satisfy a private ambition? Philosophy is not a useful science, like mathematics, requisite for engineers. It is a remnant or an echo of prophetic inspirations launched in antiquity into an ignorant world, and it perpetuates the Babel there. And as to business, if this meant the exercise of a needful profession with the necessary moderate compensation, the business man might plod on like any other artisan under a just consumer's economy. But business enterprise and free speculation are not in that class; at best they are instances of the producer's economy, which by chance may launch something valuable, or reorganise economic machinery to the ultimate public advantage; but essentially they are private adventures prompted by private ambition.

With his strong satirical intelligence and his strong aesthetic sense, I have no doubt that Green's inland voyage in China was profitable to his mind. He needed a career; he was not an ornamental young man with an ornamental culture in an ornamental society. By way of settling down, he went to the British West Indies and undertook fruit-growing. Incidentally he found there an original solution to the problem of love and marriage. He formed an uncloudedly happy union—with a Negress. This was no mere tropical interlude of sensual captivity. The lady—he showed me her photograph—was a slight little thing, not darker than some white people, and he had the greatest respect for her native wisdom and even for her literary taste. He regretted not taking her with him on his travels, but she would not have been admitted to the hotels, not at least in the United States.

All was not well, however, in that tropical paradise. Green's fruit was exceptionally good, but couldn't find a market. The United Fruit Company with its steamers wouldn't accept it: there wasn't enough of it, and it wasn't packed in the popular way. The public preferred insipid standard fruit in great beds of cotton wool to luscious special fruits in smaller baskets. Here was the tyranny of the distributor's economy persecuting the independent American in his Eden.

I have commemorated many American friends, and not one man of letters, not one poet. The poets and the learned men remained, for the most part, in the category of acquaintances. There may have been a professional feminine jealousy between us that prevented a frank and hearty comradeship. Yet I have been keeping in reserve a learned friend and poet for whom I had a great admiration, although I am not sure that it was returned, except by a certain dutiful respect for my age and for the sphere of my interests. We lived in the same garden within the same wilderness, but not with the same emotions. I cared for the garden, and he respected the wilderness. I have mentioned him before, among my younger Harvard friends: Joe or (as he afterwards called himself) Trumbull Stickney.

It is not at Harvard, however, that I like to think of him, either when he was an undergraduate or when some ten years later he returned there to teach Greek. I remember him with more pleasure in Paris during that long interval when he bloomed freely under all sorts of influences stimulating to the spirit. In his nice lodgings overlooking the quiet side of the Luxembourg gardens, or in long walks along the Seine, he would reveal his gradual change of allegiance from classic antiquity to something more troubled and warmer, more charitable, closer to the groping mind of our day, to the common people, and to the problem of America. He had been privately educated; his Latin and Greek were not of the slovenly kind that passed muster at Harvard; he spoke and wrote French beautifully. Yet except for his friend Henri Hubert, who was an archeologist and very like a German, I don't think he felt in the French the sterling qualities of his own people, nor could he tolerate the English: he was too impatient and too subtle to put up with their slow mental tempo and their moral assurance. I could never bring him to do justice to Spartan or Roman virtue. He found it brutal and stupid. I think he distrusted me also for being a materialist, not so much in theory, for we never discussed that, but in my constant sense of the animal basis of spirit, and my disrespect for any claim on the part of spirit to govern the world. He feared me. I was a Mephistopheles masquerading as a conservative. I defended the past because once it had been victorious and had brought something beautiful to light; but I had no clear expectation of better things in the future. He saw looming behind me the dreadful spectres of truth and of death.

I wonder if Stickney suspected, when he shuddered thus at my philosophy, that he was helping to quicken in me the immense sympathy that he felt for the philosophy of India. When he died his friends very kindly asked me if there was any book of his that I should like as a memento. I had vivid mementoes already: a lovely edition of Virgil that he had given me and that has filled many a vacant half-hour, always with thanks to the giver; and also his own doctor's thesis on *Les Sentences dans la Poésie Grècque,* which was an attack on rhetoric, and gave me a constant warning of the dangers I ran in that direction. Still, for a further memento, I asked for his copy—which he had once lent me—of Gade's *Die Samkyaphilosophie.* The gist of these Indian studies was given also in one of Stickney's most interesting poems. A Hindu finds himself in ancient Athens, bewildered by the noise of trade, politics and war, elbowed aside by the rude youths, forsaken and starving. At last in a quiet lane he knocks at a modest door. It is opened by a venerable old man. The stranger is introduced into a walled garden, his bowl is filled with pure rice, and he is left alone to meditate by the trickling fountain. The old man was Epicurus.

Stickney died comparatively young. When he returned to Harvard I was expecting to leave, and perhaps less interested in the life of the place than I had been in the old days, while he was busier than in Paris and preoccupied with matters not within my horizon. In any case, we seldom saw each other. When by chance we met, I felt that my society disturbed him. This would not have troubled me in itself or on my own account. I was hardened to the eclipse of friendships, and observed it without bitterness. The sun and the planets have their times for shining: we mustn't expect them to be always in our hemisphere. Yet something else did distress me in Stickney, quite for his own sake. I felt that he was forcing himself to play a part, a painful part like that of a convert who tries to live up to his new faith and to forgive his new associates for unintentionally wounding him at every turn. It is tragic in such cases to look back to the lovely familiar world that one has abandoned for being false or wicked, and to seek in vain for compensations and equivalents in the strange system that one has decided to call good and true. So Newman must have suffered when he became a Catholic. When would the ivy mantle these new brick walls, or the voice modulate the Latin liturgy as it had done the English? In some such case I imagined Stickney to find himself, now that he was back in America. His conscience had compelled him to swear allegiance to his country and to his work; but he was not at home; he had always been an exotic, warmed and watered in a greenhouse; and the harsh air and tough weeds of his native heath tried him severely. But perhaps the suffering that he endured was not due to any such moral disharmony: this may be merely my supposition. It may have been simply overwork, and the beginnings of the tumor in the brain that was about to kill him. Still that tumor itself was a sign of maladaptation. The too delicate plant, that had already flowered, couldn't endure the change of soil and of temperature, and bred a parasite that choked it.

CHAPTER VIII

OFFICIAL CAREER AT HARVARD

O N MY return to America in 1888 I at once consulted
Royce as to my thesis for the doctorate, and suggested
for a subject the philosophy of Schopenhauer, because
Schopenhauer was the German author that I liked
most and knew best. The wise Royce shook his head. That might
do, he said, for a master of arts, not for a doctor of philosophy.
Instead, he proposed Lotze. I had read Lotze's *Microcosmos* and
liked a certain moderation and orthodoxy that pervaded it, without deeply respecting its principles or its conclusions. Lotze was
a higher form of Palmer. But Royce said that his other books
were more technical and his metaphysics rather Leibnitzian. That
sounded better. I agreed, procured the complete works of Lotze,
and set to work to read, digest and annotate them, composing a
running summary and commentary, out of which my thesis might
be afterwards drawn. It was a pleasant task, not at all brain-
racking. I was soon absorbed in it, living in complete retirement
at my mother's at Roxbury. For exercise I would walk to Boston
or to Cambridge. I went to weekly seminars, admirable stimulants,
given by James and Royce. James read to us from the manuscript,
chapter by chapter, his new *Principles of Psychology*; while with
Royce we read Hegel's *Phaenomenologie des Geistes*.

I wish now that my thesis might have been on Hegel; it would
have meant harder work, and it would have been more inadequate; yet it would have prepared me better for professional con-
troversies and for understanding the mind of my time. Lotze was
stillborn, and I have forgotten everything that I then had to read
in him and to ponder. I liked Hegel's *Phaenomenologie*; it set me

planning my *Life of Reason;* and now I like even his *Logik,* not the dialectical sophistry in it, but the historical and critical lights that appear by the way. I could have written, even then, a critical thesis, say on *Logic, Sophistry, and Truth in Hegel's Philosophy.* This would have knit my own doctrine together at the beginning of my career, as I have scarcely had the chance of doing at the end. My warhorse would not have been so much blinded and hidden under his trappings.

My dull thesis on Lotze was duly accepted, and I was told that I was the most normal doctor of philosophy that they had ever created. Retrospectively I may have been, because most of the candidates had been lame ducks; but prospectively, as a doctor who teaches, I was to prove unsatisfactory and irregular. They may have suspected as much; but they were kind masters and not in a position to make great demands. They accepted me thankfully in spite of my lack of a vocation for teaching; and at once a place was made for me among them. James wished to relieve himself of his course on Locke, Berkeley, and Hume: I was invited to give it for him at a salary of $500. This was an opening, and in itself a boon. With my allowance I should have $1000 for the year. I could return to live in the Yard and (if the appointment were renewed) I could go to Europe for the summer.

On the second day that I met my class of three or four pupils, the door unexpectedly opened and in walked President Eliot, as straight and solemn as *Hamlet's* Ghost. I got up from my chair, confused but without saying audibly "Angels and ministers of grace, defend me." Eliot said dryly: "Professor Bowen has resigned. Only three students had elected his course on Descartes, Spinoza, and Leibnitz, but we don't like to suppress any course that has been announced in the elective pamphlet. I therefore have come to ask you if you would be able and willing to give that course also, in addition to this; and the payment would be the same, another $500." I replied, quite reassured: "Thank you very much. May I have until tomorrow morning to think the matter over, when I will call at your office and give you the answer?" He said that would do perfectly, and looking somewhat less ghostlike he took his leave.

I don't know how clear the rest of my lecture on the life of John Locke may have been; but somehow it came to an end: and it was easy for me, once alone and fortified with a little food, to decide that I could manage to give that other course also. I should have one lecture a day at a convenient hour in the morning. The professors whose place I was taking were old rogues and had chosen eleven o'clock, the best hour for teaching: because it gave you an hour or two before your lecture to think over your subject and look up any necessary point, and luncheon not long after. Personally that pleased me; but professionally—and I now had a competitive profession—it was disadvantageous, because that hour was occupied by half the favourite courses for undergraduates. However, a small class with graduate students in it was perhaps best for a beginning. It reduced the physical strain, as well as the already small distance between the teacher and the pupils. We could philosophise together. And financially I was set at ease. If things went on like that, I could satisfy all my tastes and requirements.

I am told that in my first years I was a very bad lecturer. Certainly my talks were desultory, not rich in information and not well arranged for taking notes. My interest was never in facts or erudition, but always in persons and ideas. I wished to re-think the thoughts of those philosophers, to understand why they took the direction they took, and then to consider the consequences and implications of taking that direction. At bottom, I was always discovering and developing my own philosophy. This at first was inarticulate, latent in me but not consistently thought out; and I can well believe that my pupils didn't understand it, and gathered only vague notions of the authors I discussed: for I doubt that the texts were much studied directly in those days at Harvard. The undergraduates were thinking only of examinations and relied on summaries in the histories of philosophy and on lecture notes. Nevertheless, even at the beginning, my pupils were attentive and friendly; and eventually my way of thinking had some influence on some of them. If they had read the texts assigned, their time on the whole would not have been wasted.

I think, however, that lectures, like sermons, are usually unprofitable. Philosophy can be communicated only by being evoked: the pupil's mind must be engaged dialectically in the discussion. Otherwise all that can be taught is the literary history of philosophy, that is, the *phrases* that various philosopheres have rendered famous. To conceive what those phrases meant or could mean would require a philosophical imagination in the public which cannot be demanded. All that usually exists is familiarity with current phrases, and a shock, perhaps of pleased curiosity but more often of alarm and repulsion, due to the heterodoxy of any different phrases.

It may be conceit on my part but I think I was the only free and disinterested thinker among the Harvard philosophers. The others were looking in philosophy either for science or for religion. They were as tolerant as I, or more so, of differences in opinion; but only as you are tolerant of all the kinds and sizes of shoes in a shop window. You are willing to have all varieties of shoes offered for selection; but you look for a single pair of shoes to choose for yourself, to pay for, to own, to wear, and to wear out or to be buried in; and you examine that vast assortment anxiously, with an unquiet mind, lest you should choose the wrong pair. Those liberal minds were thirsting for a tyrant. I, being a materialist, cynic, and Tory in philosophy, never dreamt of rebelling against the despotism of nature; and I accepted having feet, ugly and insufficient as they might be, because it would be much worse not to have them. But as to shoes, I have and mean to keep a free mind, and would be willing to go barefoot if it were convenient or if it were the fashion. So I believe, compulsorily and satirically, in the existence of this absurd world; but as to the existence of a better world, or of hidden reasons in this one, I am incredulous, or rather, I am critically sceptical; because it is not difficult to see the familiar motives that lead men to invent such myths. So I survey all those high-heeled ladies' shoes and all those invalids' fur-lined slippers with a smile: I might have worn the first once in some masquerade, and may yet wear the second in my decrepitude; but they are accidental paraphernalia. So are all systems of philosophy, so are all logical languages, so are all allegories and images of sense. The study of them is a part of the humanities, initiating us into the history of human life and mind; it is not the pursuit of science or salvation.

This divergence between me and my environment was not merely one of opinion: it interfered with my career and with the natural growth of my mind. President Eliot, who was an anti-humanist, once said to me that we should teach the *facts*, not merely convey *ideas*. I might have replied that the only facts in philosophy were historical facts, namely, the fact that people had or had had certain ideas. But of course I only smiled and took note of *his idea*. The history of philosophy is the only philosophy that should be taught in a university. Systems of philosophy are taught only by sects or by individuals setting out to be prophets and to found a sect. I now have a system of philosophy which I hadn't dreamt of then, although the reasons for it lay all in me; but this system is not intended to found a sect and will never do so. It aspires to be only a contribution to the humanities, the expression of a reflective, selective, and free mind. But I was living among sects, or among individuals eager to found sects; and I should have seemed to them vague and useless if I had been merely a historian and critic in philosophy. I was expected and almost compelled to be "constructive" or "creative," or to pretend to be so. Or as they put it, I must take up some special subject, physiological psychology (supposed to be a science) or Greek philosophy, if I trained myself to write a history, like Zeller's. A man must have a "specialty."

I was a kind of poet, I was alive to architecture and the other arts, I was at home in several languages: "aesthetics" might be regarded as my specialty. Very well: although I didn't have, and haven't now, a clear notion of what "aesthetics" may be, I undertook to give a course in that subject. It would help to define my status. I gave it for one or two years and then I wrote out the substance of it in a little book: *The Sense of Beauty*. The manuscript of this book went from local publisher to publisher, and was rejected. I had given up all expectation of getting it published when Barrett Wendell, always friendly to me and the humanities, sent me word that he thought Scribner's would accept it. I sent it to Scribner's; it was printed and did not prove a financial loss to the publisher, although it had neither a large sale nor a warm reception from the critics. However, it was a book, *a fact*; and it established pleasant relations between me and Scribner's which have lasted for fifty years.

My sham course in "Aesthetics" had served its purpose and so had my little book. Although looked at askance by the President I was reappointed year by year, and then for three years at a time with a salary of $1500 and a seat in the Faculty, which I seldom occupied. My life and pleasures were still those of a student; I lived on intimate terms with a knot of undergraduates; I went to "parties," chiefly dinner parties in Boston. In time I undertook another "constructive" or "creative" course entitled "Philosophy of History": this title attracted larger numbers, perhaps thirty men, many of them Jews: and it prepared the ground for my *Life of Reason*. But what then most enticed me in philosophy was Plato, and I had always had a great respect for Aristotle, especially for his *Ethics* and *Politics*; and out of these, with the help of a glance at Bacon, Locke, Montesquieu, and Taine (authors that my pupils could be expected to read a little) I composed my lectures on the "philosophy of history," which for me meant no providential plan of creation or redemption, but merely retrospective politics; a study of what had formed the chief interests of mankind in various epochs. Religion—my strong point in history—naturally came in, and I treated it, I think, without giving offence in any quarter.

In the winter and spring of 1896 I became convinced that the time had come for calling a halt. I had been an instructor for seven years: should I ask for promotion or look for another place? In my private life too there had come a crisis: my young friends had become too young for me and I too old for them; I had made a private peace with all religions and philosophies; and I had grown profoundly weary of polite society and casual gaieties. Then it chanced that at the English Cambridge they had established a new category of "advanced students," and Lowes Dickinson and Nathaniel Wedd of King's College had suggested that I might be admitted there. Here was an opportunity to break away from my second college life, already too much prolonged, yet continue my academic career, study Greek philosophy, live a while in England, and in the holidays re-visit Italy more at leisure than in 1895. I therefore asked Eliot for a year's leave of absence without a salary, after which I would return to Harvard for one more year; and then, unless I were appointed assistant professor, I should look for a place elsewhere.

This project was carried out. When I returned to America in September 1897, I settled down at my mother's, now no longer at Roxbury but in Longwood, within walking distance of Harvard. Electric cars were also available. It was a most economical way of living, practically with no expense except for luncheon, fifty cents at the Colonial Club. My relations with undergraduates and with Boston society, although renewed, were renewed on a new basis. I no longer played the familiar companion or the young man about town. I was simply an elderly mentor or an occasional guest. I began to give a new course, Philosophy 12, on Plato and Aristotle in English, which remained my chief subject until almost the end. I lectured on the *Republic,* the *Phaedras,* the *Symposium,* the *Phaedo* and the *Nicomachaean Ethics.* These books were assigned to be read in translation; and the essays submitted to me upon them by my pupils, usually not twenty in number, were sometimes excellent. I have given an imaginary fragment of one of them in *The Last Puritan.*

Early in 1898 I was appointed assistant professor for five years, at $2000 a year. When this appointment expired, it was renewed on the usual terms; but actually it ran only for four years, when at last I was made a full professor, with a salary of $4000. More-over, two of those four years, 1904–1906, I spent abroad: the first, a sabbatical year, in Italy and the East, the second at Paris as exchange professor at the Sorbonne. This second lap of my assistant professorship was therefore much pleasanter and more varied than the first: and the last lap of all, during the four and a half years of my active professorship, also passed imperceptibly: I knew they were the last lap, and the exhilaration of finishing the race, even if not with an outward victory, was an inward comfort.

My official career at Harvard was thus completed without a break. When I resigned my professorship my name had figured in the Harvard Catalogue, in one capacity or another, for thirty years. Yet that long career had been slow and insecure, made in an atmosphere of mingled favour and distrust. My relations with President Eliot and with other influential persons had always been strained. I had disregarded or defied public opinion by not be-coming a specialist, but writing pessimistic, old-fashioned verses, continuing to range superficially over literature and philosophy, being indiscernibly a Catholic or an atheist, attacking Robert Browning, prophet of the half-educated and half-believing, avoid-ing administrative duties, neglecting the intelligentsia, frequenting the society of undergraduates and fashionable ladies, spending my holidays abroad, and even appearing as a witness in the disrepu-table Russell trial. At the same time, in private, I had breathed the pleasantest airs of sympathy and friendship. My philosophic colleagues had supported me, my old friends had been faithful, appreciative, and always hospitable, my new friends had multi-plied in numbers and influence, my books, though received coldly at first, had attained a certain reputation. I was still disliked, but I was swallowed.

Harvard, in those the waning days of Eliot's administration, was getting out of hand. Instruction was every day more multi-farious and more chaotic; athletics and college life developed vigorously as they chose, yet not always pleasantly; and the Graduate and associated Schools worked each in its own way, with only nominal or financial relations with Harvard College. In public opinion a reaction was beginning to appear; but it had not taken visible form before the change of Presidents. Government was monarchical; but a monarch can hardly decide everything on his own initiative; he depends on vested interests and traditional advisers for his policy, and on committees and agents for carrying it out. Eliot, autocrat as he was, depended on the Fellows, half a dozen business men in Boston who were the legal proprietors of Harvard, and especially on one of them, the Treasurer, who managed the vast investments of the Foundation. He was also somewhat controlled by the Board of Overseers, elected representatives of the graduates. All this formed an immense tangle of disconnected activities: the President was driving not a four but a forty-in-hand. Most numerous and stately, but tamest, in this working menagerie was the Faculty of Arts and Sciences. Although a member of it, I hardly knew what were its attributions or privileges. The most interesting and clearest business of the meetings was to hear what the President might tell us of the action or prospects of the moment; and it was from him that any likely measures emanated. Sometimes, very rarely, there was clear opposition or even a hostile vote. That might produce a postponement, but could hardly arrest the movement of reform that he had undertaken in the interest of democratic arrangements and quick returns. Education meant preparation for professional life. College, and all that occupied the time and mind of the College, and seemed to the College an end in itself, seemed to President Eliot only a means. The end was service in the world of business.

The Faculty meetings were an object lesson to me in the futility of parliamentary institutions. Those who spoke spoke badly, with imperfect knowledge of the matter in hand, and simply to air their prejudices. The rest hardly listened. If there was a vote, it revealed not the results of the debate, but the previous and settled sentiments of the voters. The uselessness and the poor quality of the whole performance were so evident that it surprised me to see that so many intelligent men—for they were intelligent when doing their special work—should tamely waste so much time in keeping up the farce. But parliamentary institutions have a secret function in the Anglo-Saxon world, like those important glands that seem useless to a superficial anatomy. There is an illusion of self-government, especially for members of the majority; there is a gregarious sense of safety and reassurance in being backed, or led, or even opposed by crowds of your equals under conventional safeguards and guarantees; and there is solace to the vague mind in letting an anonymous and irresponsible majority be responsible for everything. You grumble but you consent to put up with the course that things happen to take. It is not as if the ruling party had intended the result: they gave a little push, and evolution has done the rest.

The Harvard Faculty was not divided into parties. Being appointed by the President, who was the irremovable executive, they were more like officials, naturally respectful to their chief; but some of them had personal views on education and public policy which they couldn't refrain from airing in voting on the President's reforms. I seldom went to the meetings, and spoke only once, when asked a direct question touching a degree to be granted out of course to an absent undergraduate, Bayard Cutting, who had left college to be private secretary to the American Ambassador in London, and had written a thesis on David Hume as a substitute for his unfinished work. I had read the thesis, and gave my opinion on it. The degree was granted. Bayard Cutting had been one of my young friends at the time when, to my sense, they were birds of passage. He married Lady Sybil Cuffe, who after his death lived in the Villa Medici, close to Strong's villa at Fiesole. Their only child, Iris, who herself lost her only child, wrote a book on Leopardi, for which she asked me to supply a "Foreword." It is a strange sadness that hangs for me now over all that history. An international intelligentsia adrift amid unsuspected currents and wrecked one by one on the reefs of El Dorado.

Did the members of the Harvard Faculty form an intellectual society? Had they any common character or influence? I think not. In the first place they were too much overworked, too poor, too much tied up in their modest homes. Nor had they had, like old-fashioned English dons, a common education, and written Latin hexameters and pentameters. I believe there were some dinner clubs or supper clubs among the elder professors: but I never heard of any idea or movement springing up among them, or any literary fashion. It was an anonymous concourse of coral insects, each secreting one cell, and leaving that fossil legacy to enlarge the earth.

Beyond my philosophical colleagues I had hardly any acquaintances among the professors, except Professor Toy, because of his wife, who was a friend and frequent hostess of mine for many years. Even among the younger teachers I had few friends. One, however, stood in a position very much like mine, in that teaching at Harvard was for him a sort of expedient, rather than a chosen profession, and that his interests and the subject he taught touched European history and politics. "Archie" Coolidge, as he was called, had been booked for a diplomatic career, and was actually secretary to some Legation, I believe in Vienna, when for a private reason he threw up his post and returned to Boston. He had been engaged to be married, and the young lady, in his absence, had changed her mind. The poor man, who was deeply in love, lost his head completely, and thought that by personal protestations he could bring her round. Unfortunately, Archie's person was his weak point. He had family, money, intelligence, experience and accomplishments, spoke even Russian, and had travelled all over the world. When I once asked him why he was going to Kamchatka he replied, "I haven't yet been there." But in his physique and manner, though there was nothing markedly wrong, he seemed not quite normal, as if nature had put him together carelessly with insufficient materials, and had managed to make him go, but only by fits and jerks. And his mind, too, while well stocked and perfectly reasonable, seemed somehow thin, as if there were no central sun in it, no steady light and centre of gravity. Anyhow, his return only made matters worse: he had left his post without excuse or permission and couldn't resume it. To fill up his time and to try to distract his mind from his terrible disappointment, people suggested that he should teach for a while at Harvard. In these circumstances he came to live in Cambridge, ate at the Colonial Club, and gathered a circle of young friends about him who were often my friends too. In these ways we were thrown together. We had a common *milieu* at Harvard and a common outlook into the great world, and his wider information always lent interest to what he said; but whether because of diplomatic reserve or of having a purely documentary mind, he never betrayed his deeper allegiance in politics and morals. American diplomacy was as yet innocent, an entertaining sport or holiday for home politicians; at most a little commercial or missionary enterprise might be connected with it. My relations with Archie Coolidge therefore remained always pleasant and unimportant.

Of the older Harvard worthies I was on good terms with two, Charles Eliot Norton and William James. They were perhaps the most distinguished, but not the most trusted; they too had had to be swallowed. They too, although in my time their position was established, had seemed at first questionable and irregular. Norton, with ten generations of local magnates behind him, had his inspirations and sympathies far away. He worshipped Greek art, he worshipped Christian art, he loved refined English life. He spoke rarefied English. He loved Turner and Ruskin. His personal friends were Burne-Jones, Carlyle and Matthew Arnold. To me he showed the most exquisite paternal kindness. He encouraged and praised me whenever he could do so conscientiously: when he wished to warn or admonish me, he did it through his nephew, Frank Bullard, who was one of my best friends. He feared that I lived too much among dreams. When my extravagant drama, *Lucifer,* was published, I of course sent him a copy; and in thanking me he said that the value of it, in its substance, could not be known for the present, but that the versification was that of a master. This was flattery, but not absurd flattery, from an old man with Victorian standards in literature. "Versification" was the right word in this case, for mine is not what English-speaking people now call poetry: it is not a dissolution and fresh concretion of language. Verbally it is ordinary speech made rhythmical and harmonious. Where I break through convention, whether in verse or prose, is in my themes or sentiments, as here in *Lucifer*. Norton very modestly and prudently refused to judge on this point. He was not at home in metaphysics or religion; the dissolution of common sense and a fresh concretion of myths seemed to him, I suspect, a waste of time. Here he had the prejudices of a positivist; yet he was cultivated and courteous enough to conceal them when speaking to a young man, like me, who possessed imagination without trusting it to reveal truth. My scepticism reconciled him to my mythology, and made him more benevolent than he might have been to a fanatic; and he was always benevolent, even when grieved.

At the funeral of C. C. Everett, an old professor at the Harvard Divinity School, a Unitarian and a Fichtean, I happened to join Norton as we came out. "All this," he said with his usual sweetness, "must make a sad impression on you." I admitted that of course death was sad, but my acquaintance with Everett had been very slight, and it was not, at his age, a loss to our philosophical forces. "I don't mean the death of Dr. Everett. He was a good man, but he had no intellect-u-al power" (Norton pronounced with this extreme accuracy, but easily; and the habit sometimes gave a satirical force to his words). "What I meant," he continued, "was this survival of superstition among us. Mr. Cruthers has compared Dr. Everett to an eagle." Cruthers was the Unitarian minister in Cambridge and couldn't help being saturated with complacency and with unctuous flattery of everything mediocre; but he was hardly superstitious. To compare that old theological or anti-theological professor to St. John was absurd or, if you like, blasphemous: but the primary evil was the insensibility to St. John, not the obituary fulsomeness about Everett. Fulsomeness and complete lack of perspective had become habitual in American appreciation of Americans. There was a conspiracy of flattery; free lances were sometimes broken against it, but the phalanx might be expected to sweep the field, and to form public opinion. This, I think, was what made Norton sad.

Norton was president of the Tavern Club, which occasionally gave dinners in compliment to some person not a member. I recollect two such occasions on which Norton presided, and made the inevitable complimentary speech. Here he ran serious danger of falling into the "superstition" that saddened him in others. But he had a means of safety; he was not without wit, a mild irony that saved him from platitudes. One dinner was in honour of John Fiske, a local disciple of Herbert Spencer, who had passed from popular science to history, and published first a book on *Cosmic Evolution* and later a *History of the United States*. Norton, in his speech, after paddling about as usual in the backwaters of anecdote, said that Fiske had been an industrious author. "I wish his style had been a little chastened,[1] but the substance has been solid. He began by giving us a history of the universe; he proceeded to give us a history of the United States; and we may hope that in this upward progress he may end by giving us a history of Cambridge, Massachusetts." The distrust of speculative pretensions, the positivism, the love of home and country (which was profound in Norton, and the cause of his melancholy) were all expressed in these words, with which he ended his speech.

The other dinner was in honour of Rudyard Kipling. Hard luck for Norton, I thought at first; why hadn't he pretended to be ill and let someone else praise what must be odious to him? But not at all. Norton was quite happy, not in his remarks but in his mood. He had known and liked Kipling's mother, and he was prepared *a priori* to accept the bard of imperialism as a distinguished lover of humanity. Kipling sympathised with the Hindus; he was democratic; a glib prophet with warm feelings and popular

[1] Norton said "chassened," doubtless to indicate that the word means castigated and not made chaste.

rhythms; and Norton was so saturated with morality that when anything seemed to him morally right, he couldn't notice whether it was vulgar. That which seemed paramount in Norton, his fastidious retrospective nostalgia, was in reality secondary. Fundamental still was his fidelity to the conscience of his ancestors.

Concerning William James, I have made sundry scattered observations for the public without attempting a fair total portrayal of the man or of his philosophy: neither he nor his philosophy lent themselves to being summed up. But here, where I am portraying only my own impressions, I may add a word more about the feelings that he excited in me. I trusted his heart but I didn't respect his judgment. I admired his masculine directness, his impressionistic perceptions, and his picturesque words. I treasured his utterances on the medical side of things, such as that the best way to understanding the normal is to study the abnormal. All this belonged to his independent, radical, naturalistic temper, to his American sense of being just born into a world to be rediscovered. But he was really far from free, held back by old instincts, subject to old delusions, restless, spasmodic, self-interrupted: as if some impetuous bird kept flying aloft, but always stopped in mid-air, pulled back with a jerk by an invisible wire tethering him to a peg in the ground. The general agreement in America to praise him as a marvellous person, and to pass on, is justified by delight at the way he started, without caring where he went. In fact, he got nowhere; and for that reason his influence could be great and beneficent over those who knew him, but soon seemed to become untraceable in the confused currents of the world. I, for instance, was sure of his goodwill and kindness, of which I had many proofs; but I was also sure that he never understood me, and that when he talked to me there was a manikin in his head, called G. S. and entirely fantastic, which he was addressing. No doubt I profited materially by this illusion, because he would have liked me less if he had understood me better; but the sense of that illusion made spontaneous friendship impossible. I was uncomfortable in his presence. He was so extremely

natural that there was no knowing what his nature was, or what
to expect next; so that one was driven to behave and talk conven-
tionally, as in the most artificial society. I found no foothold, I
was soon fatigued, and it was a relief to be out again in the open,
and alone.

The feeling of walking on quicksands became almost worse
when what he said was in harmony with my feelings than when
it was opposed to them. If he talked about ghosts, I didn't care
what turn his fancy might take; he would surely be graphic if he
described those ghosts dramatically, and he would not in the least
disturb me if he suggested that they might now be stealthily
gliding behind our chairs. When, on the contrary, he said something that seemed to corroborate my own sentiments, I feared a
trap. Let me describe one instance. One afternoon in the autumn
of 1898 we were standing in Palmer's library after a brief business
meeting, and conversation turned on the terms of peace imposed
by the United States on Spain after the Cuban war. James was
terribly distressed. Addressing himself rather to Palmer, who was
evidently enjoying the pleasant rays of the setting sun on his back,
and the general spacious comfort of his library (he then lived in
the old President's house at the corner of Quincy Street), James
said he felt he had lost his country. Intervention in Cuba might
be defended, on account of the perpetual bad government there
and the sufferings of the natives. But the annexation of the Philippines, what could excuse that? What could be a more shameless
betrayal of American principles? What could be a plainer symptom of greed, ambition, corruption and imperialism? Palmer smiled
approvingly, yet he saw the other side. Every thesis has its antithesis: the synthesis would be ultimately for the general good,
and the course of history was the true Judgment of God. Those
were not his words, but his little vague commonplaces could be
so interpreted by anyone behind the scenes.

As for me, I couldn't help resenting the schoolmaster's manner
of the American government, walking switch in hand into a neighbour's garden to settle the children's quarrels there, and to make

himself master of the place. Yet that has been the way of the world since the beginning of time, and if anything could be reasonably complained of, it was the manner of the intrusion rather than the fact of it. For me the tragedy lay in Spanish weakness rather than in American prepotency: Uncle Sam would have continued to regard all men as free and equal, if all other men had looked as strong as himself. Yet Spanish weakness comes only of Quixotic frailty, due to tragic and comic disproportion between the spirit and the flesh. The resources of the country and people would not be materially contemptible if they were wisely husbanded, and devoted to developing at home, under native inspiration, an austere, passionate and intelligent life for the soul. The Spanish empire overseas had been glorious enough, and the end, harshly as it grazed against my family memories, seemed to me almost a relief. I am not one of those who dream of a Spanish America subject in future to the influence of the mother country. Let Spanish America, I say, and let English America be as original as they can: what is best in Spain, as what is best in England, cannot migrate.

I was therefore much more at peace about this pathetic war than was William James, or than was "Aunt Sarah," whom I had visited in the previous June, on my way to Europe. She, the mother of the heroic Colonel Shaw of the Massachusetts coloured regiment, even before there was talk of the Philippines was scandalised at McKinley. A large American flag was hanging in the street opposite her windows. "I wish I could pull that down!" she cried, condescending a little perhaps to my Spanish sympathies, but chiefly moved by the betrayal, as she thought it, of true American principles. "No, no," I protested, "the thing is sad for Spain, but was inevitable sooner or later. McKinley is only yielding to *force majeure*." Nor was I alone in this feeling. When the armistice was announced, I ran down to Avila from Paris. As we approached the frontier a merry crowd of young trippers, well-dressed men and girls, filled the train with laughter and shrill cries; they were Spanish people on an excursion to San Sebastian for the bullfight. At Irun I was not even asked for my passport. And in Avila I found everybody as resigned and sadly philosophical as I, or as any ancient sage.

Why was William James so much upset by an event that the victims of it could take so calmly? Because he held a false moralistic view of history, attributing events to the conscious ideals and free will of individuals: whereas individuals, especially in governments, are creatures of circumstance and slaves to vested interests. These interests may be more or less noble, romantic, or sordid, but they inevitably entangle and subjugate men of action. The leaders couldn't act or maintain themselves at the head of affairs if they didn't engage the impulses at work in the mass, or in some part of it. Catastrophes come when some dominant institution, swollen like a soap bubble and still standing without foundations, suddenly crumbles at the touch of what may seem a word or an idea, but is really some stronger material force. This force is partly that of changing circumstances, partly that of changing passions, but passions are themselves physical impulses, maturing in their season, and often epidemic, like contagious diseases. James, who was a physician and a pragmatist, might have been expected to perceive this, and did perceive it at moments: yet the overruling tradition in him was literary and theological, and he cried disconsolately that he had lost his country, when his country, just beginning to play its part in the history of the world, appeared to ignore an ideal that he had innocently expected would always guide it, because this ideal had been eloquently expressed in the Declaration of Independence. But the Declaration of Independence was a piece of literature, a salad of illusions. Admiration for the noble savage, for the ancient Romans (whose republic was founded on slavery and war), mixed with the quietistic maxims of the Sermon on the Mount, may inspire a Rousseau but it cannot guide a government. The American Colonies were rehearsing independence and were ready for it. That was what gave to the Declaration of Independence its timeliness and political weight. In 1898 the United States were rehearsing domination over tropical America and were ready to organise and to legalise it; it served their commercial and military interests and their imaginative passions. Such antecedents and such facilities made intervention sooner or later inevitable. Domination was the implicit aim, whatever might be the language or even the thoughts of individuals. William James had not lost his country; his country was in good health and just reaching the age of puberty. He had merely lost his way in its physiological history.

James's displeasure at the seizure of the Philippines was therefore, from my point of view, merely accidental. It did not indicate any sympathy with Spain, or with anything in history that interests and delights me. On the contrary, it was an expression of principles entirely opposed to mine; much more so than the impulses of young, ambitious, enterprising America. These impulses may ignore or even insult all that I most prize, but they please me nevertheless for their honest enthusiasm and vitality. James himself, like a good American, was full of honest enthusiasm and vitality, and besides was sensitive, learned, and a perfect gentleman. In him too I sympathised with the initial phases and moral promptings of his thoughts. The bird flew up bravely; but when my eye was able to follow his flight, I saw him flutter, and perch, as if he had lost his energy, on some casual bough. His inspiration, even in science, was that of romanticism.

Less distinguished than Norton or James were two or three stray souls in official Harvard with whom I inwardly sympathised, perhaps without much personal contact. They too were barely tolerated by the authorities; they had cut peep-holes, as it were, in the sacred tabernacle through which to view the natural landscape. One of these was Barrett Wendell. He belonged to a little group of free spirits, almost of wits, in the Harvard class of 1877, and had been one of the founders of the *Lampoon*. His affections were local and his ideals conservative. He allowed himself little eccentricities, had tricks of intonation mistaken by many for an attempt to speak like the English; he admired the airs of the early nineteenth century, cared for birth and good breeding,

and in literature for mannishness and good form, "rum and de-
corum," as he once put it, and for tenderness and distinction of
feeling. Yet he had no real distinction himself; his mind and his
attachments, like his speech, were explosive and confused; there
was emotion, often deep emotion, but it broke out in ill-governed
and uncouth ways. He was not at all an Anglomaniac: he idealised only the old colonial proprieties and dignities: he longed
for an American aristocracy, not of millionaires, but of local
worthies, sportsmen, scholars and divines. The New England
literary men and orators of fifty years before would have satisfied
him in respect to their station and manners, but he detested the
radical revolutionary turn of their minds. He hated the empty,
cold self-sufficiency, as he thought it, of Emerson and his friends.
They had desiccated and impoverished the heart; they had made
the world less passionate and less interesting to live in. In a word,
Wendell was a sentimentalist.

Had he been thoroughly educated and a good Latinist like Dr.
Johnson, he might have expressed and propagated his ideals to
better purpose; as it was, his force spent itself in foam. He was a
good critic of undergraduate essays; but not a fair historian or a
learned man; and his books were not worth writing. He was useful
in the College as a pedagogue, and there was a certain moral
stimulus in his original personality. He carried his little person
jauntily; wore spats and a red beard; when walking he would
brandish the stick that (like me) he always carried; he would
perpetually twirl the signet at the end of his watch-chain. Something admirable was wasted in him. The age made it impossible
for him to do well what he would have loved to do.

Why should such a man ever dream of becoming a professor?
His case, I imagine, was not unlike mine. He happened to have
his pigeon-hole in Boston, he was not rich, he liked to browse
upon belles-lettres; why not teach English composition and literature at Harvard? But with science and President Eliot in control,
would Harvard accept his services? It was long very much in
doubt. With time, however, Wendell had become a familiar

figure, an object of universal smiles and affection; and when the official guillotine was ready to fall, public sentiment couldn't allow it. Indeed, in what remained of the old-fashioned College, Wendell's was useful work. He devised and carried out the plan of reading and revising hundreds of "daily themes," each on a half-sheet of note-paper: a voluntary exercise in writing, feeling, and judging of all things like a gentleman. You learned nothing except what to think about what you happened to know. If the effects of this training could spread and assert themselves against the self-confidence of the illiterate, a great change would appear in the tone of American publications. A change of tone there has certainly been in the last thirty years; and who knows how much of it may not be due to Barrett Wendell?

I seldom came across Wendell in Boston, but he was an inevitable speaker at Harvard meetings and dinners. Yet I think that silently we essentially understood each other. We were on the same side of the barricade. More than once he took some step, quite without my knowledge, to do me a kindness. Perhaps the most tangible sign of this sympathy between us was our common affection for Harvard—for the College, not for the University. We knew that the traditional follies there present were the normal, boyish, almost desirable follies of youth; and that the *virtu* there fostered and admired was genuine *virtu*, not perhaps useful for anything further, but good and beautiful in itself. We both desired to screen those follies and to propagate that *virtu* against the steam-roller of industrial democracy. We were not asking much; for these were precisely the follies and the *virtu* that democracy, if liberated from the steam-roller, would cultivate of its own accord. What we deprecated was only that this spontaneous life of the people should be frustrated by the machinery of popular government and of incorporated private interests.

A more pathetic servant of popular joys, humbler than Barrett Wendell and more openly sentimental, was my neighbour for years in the Yard, and although I seldom saw him, I was always vaguely aware of his beneficent existence round the corner. He was known as Charley Copeland. An artist rather than a scholar, he was a public reader by profession, an elocutionist; he could move his audiences by declaiming, with disciplined voice and restrained emotion, all the most touching or thrilling popular selections from the Bible to Kipling. This was a spiritual debauch for the hungry souls of the many well-disposed waifs at Harvard living under difficult conditions: and these Copeland made his special friends. Apart from his readings, he took pains to thaw out the most timid and warm them at his fire, materially and morally. He was the poor boys' providential host and inspirer, doing for the forlorn and disinherited what Norton did for those who were, or ought to have been, already somewhat cultivated, or what Palmer did, more speculatively, for the intellectual proletariat. This task of attracting the mass into the vortex of public interests, which at Yale was done by college organisations, at Harvard was done in these discreet ways by individual philanthropists, more from above and more tenderly, but I fear less successfully: because these contacts, for the majority, left only stray memories without establishing permanent personal interests. Copeland was not left without his reward in the esteem and affection of a particular circle, and of scattered admirers, yet his charitable work for the College remained for years without official recognition. It was only under President Lowell that he was made a professor.

Somewhat on the margin of Harvard lingered also for a time my friend Pierre la Rose. He too was connected with the English Department; but he pieced out his work there by planning restorations of old houses, or decorating and refurnishing them. He had excellent taste, not too servile or pedantic about the style of any period; his joy, I think, would have been like mine, in bolder decorative effects such as we were regaled with later by the Russian ballet. He was expert none the less in distinguishing the merits of classic and severe styles, and of the corresponding litera-ture, particularly the French. Unfortunately there was nothing classical or severe about his own figure; he was not looked on with favour by the undergraduates of his own time, except by other exceptional persons like Trumbull Stickney, with whom he used to play classical music, for he also had some talent in that direction; but later local prejudice against him was vanquished by his pleasant conversation, discretion and varied knowledge. I found him in my later Harvard years the most sympathetic of friends. We often sat at the same table in the small room at the Colonial Club, and if the food was negative, we had a bottle of claret, and not only Harvard, official and unofficial, but the whole literary and political world, for our intellectual bill of fare. He would have made an excellent permanent Tutor in a genuine college, not only in English composition, but in French and in comparative literature, as well as in the history of the fine arts: and had President Lowell's "Houses" existed in the 1890's, he would doubtless have made a place for himself there. He had a quiet, well-informed, unexaggerated devotion to all charming things, a devotion that teaches by contagion, and awakens a taste for what is worth loving.

I had a hearty academic friend also at Yale; and when I say that it was William Lyon Phelps, those who knew him will understand the reason, because he was the hearty friend of everybody. He had come to Harvard when a graduate student to study early English under Professors Child and Kittredge, not to speak of Barrett Wendell, whose hearty friend he instantly became, in spite of the contrast in their idiosyncrasies. My friendship with Phelps would not have become so warm, at least on my side, but for the place and moment in which it was cemented. In 1892, he had returned to Yale, became an instructor or professor there, married, and settled in a nice little house where he was immensely happy, and where there was a spare room for a guest; and knowing my recently acquired taste for contemplating athletic contests, he asked me to come and visit him and his wife for the Harvard-Yale game. I knew nothing of Yale, which for a Harvard man was a half-mythical, half-hostile invisible object. Here was a capital chance to unveil the mystery, and see something of Yale from the inside. And I didn't go alone. Warwick Potter, who had a

Groton friend at Yale, arranged to come with me; but we parted on reaching New Haven, each being met and carried off by his respective host; and we had entirely different aspects of Yale to describe, as on the Sunday afternoon we travelled back to Cambridge.

That was at the high tide of my second College period. Teaching philosophy had become a decent means of livelihood, and was not yet a burden; I was not pledged to it, and was writing nothing but poetry. Yale, seen under the enthusiastic guidance of my *cicerone,* seemed a most living, organic, distinctive, fortunate place, a toy Sparta to match our toy Athens at Harvard. I liked it very much: what is more, I *believed* in it. That was the direction in which the anonymous, gregarious mind of America could be sympathetically brought to become distinct and integral. Harvard liberalism tended, on the contrary, to encourage dissolution, intellectual and moral, under a thin veneer of miscellaneous knowledge. Phelps was naturally pleased at seeing me so sympathetic. Not considering that I was fundamentally a Spaniard and a Catholic, he thought he had converted me to muscular Christianity; and in fact he had converted me to something Christian, namely, to charity even towards muscular Americanism.

The Yale that Phelps showed me was the official Yale, yet the officials seemed to be of an extraordinarily informal, varied and youthful type. Phelps himself had these characteristics; and his wife added a gentle harmonising treble to his spontaneous baritone. I was keyed up by them to such an appreciative mood that I liked even the Y.M.C.A. I felt that it was not meddlesome, but truly friendly and helpful; and this was not the only time that I felt this among the Evangelicals. Mrs. Palmer, for instance (unlike her husband), inspired me with immediate confidence and respect. I was sure that she was honestly a friend of life in others, even when their life was not at all like hers; and when still at school I had discovered the same gift of steady charity in the much-loved Bayley. The great point was that these people should not be themselves flabby or sentimental or followers of Rousseau;

then their charity might be a true virtue, not a licence for their pet vices.

Phelps was irresistible. His every word was a cocktail, or at least a temperance drink. He made you love everything. Even if you were not naturally genial you found you were his friend, almost his intimate friend, without having in the least expected it. Whether this mesmerisation should be altogether welcome to a moralist, I am not sure. I suppose (when Phelps was not present) the most hearty optimist might distinguish degrees of delight. He might say: I delight in bread, but I delight more in bread and butter, and still more in cake; and I delight in a *baba-au-rhum* even more than in dry cake. Yet if you allow yourself to make these odious comparisons, you cast a shadow of inferiority over all delights except the greatest. You might even suspect that the greatest might some day be overshadowed, and that you might mysteriously find yourself preferring not to eat anything. Life and the morality that regulates life seem to require discrimination. They would relax, they would positively dissolve, if delight were spread indiscriminately over an infinite miscellany of commonplaces and there were nothing that you didn't love, nothing that you invincibly hated. So that perhaps the irresistible Phelps would have been too much of a good thing for all the year round; but for an occasional visit to Yale, or an occasional afternoon in Paris (where he and his wife often turned up), he was all Browning in a nutshell, and better for that compression.

It is an error into which too much domestic luxury has led American taste that all bread should be buttered. When eaten alone, bread is improved by a little butter or a little cheese, to lend it softness or savour; but when bread itself is an accompaniment, butter is out of place. It only adds grease to the greasy sauces and cloys the meat that it might have saved from cloying. So with moral enthusiasm. Great, solid, fruitful excellence should provoke it, not mere existence. Existence is something haphazard, and a great risk: the possibility of something good with the peril of many evils. Phelps complained that in my *Last Puritan* there was not a single *good* person. I thought Oliver, the Vicar, Irma, and several of the minor characters decidedly good people, and many others good enough as this world goes; but none were *merely* good, because goodness is an attribute and not a substance. To be good morally you must first be distinct physically: you must not be an anonymous *it.* The trouble with the goodness that Phelps wanted and possessed was that it was not distinguished. It seemed to me at Yale as if enthusiasm were cultivated for its own sake, as flow of life, no matter in what direction. It meant intoxication, not choice. You were not taught to attain anything capable of being kept, a treasure to be laid up in heaven. You were trained merely to succeed. And in order to be sure to succeed, it was safer to let the drift of the times dictate your purposes. Make a strong pull and a long pull and a pull all together for the sake of togetherness. Then you will win the race. A young morality, a morality of preparation, of limbering up. "Come on, fellows," it cried. "Let's see who gets there first. Rah, rah, rah! Whoop-her-up! Onward, Christian Soldier!" Irresistible as Phelps was, my nature reacted against that summons. Before I cry onward, I would inquire where I am bound. Before I take up arms, I must know in what cause. Before I call myself a Christian, I must understand what Christianity is and what it would impose upon me. Does it cry to me, as at Yale, "Come on, fellows! Let's see who gets there first!" "There," for a Christian, used to mean yonder, above, *Jenseits,* heaven: but when this world has become so lovely, and effort and work are a crown in themselves, the struggle becomes a crab race, and the real winner is he who runs forever and never gets there at all. As Emerson said, "If God is anywhere, he is here," so this modern Christian should say, If heaven isn't here it's nowhere. A conclusion that in some sense I should be willing to accept, only that I shouldn't call it Christianity: rather Epicurean contentment in being an accident in an accident.

My visits to Yale were unofficial, but I was asked to give odd lectures at most of the other New England colleges, and always did so with pleasure. My ·hosts were kind, the places, with my early memories of the Latin School and of simple old Harvard, were pleasantly reminiscent, and the intellectual atmosphere was honest and unpretending. I also gave lectures at Columbia, where the professors of philosophy took a professional interest in my views, such as in general I expect nobody to take: only perhaps a momentary pleasure in some phrase or in some bit of literary criticism. This was what came to me, by way of incense, from the female audiences that I often addressed at Radcliffe, at Wellesley, and other women's colleges. At Bryn Mawr, a comparatively fashionable place where I spoke in the Chapel, I overheard, as I came in, a loud and disappointed whisper: "He is bald!" and at Berkeley, where the summer school seemed to have no men in it, a lady observed that I had "a mellifluous voice," but that she "didn't like my logic." In the Middle West I was more honoured, even giving once the Baccalaureate Address, and at Wisconsin being welcomed twice and receiving an honorary degree. The moral and intellectual atmosphere everywhere in the United States seemed to be uniform: earnest, meagre, vague, scattered, and hopeful. After I left America, however, I gather that a sharp change occurred, introducing more variety, more boldness and greater achievements.

My academic career also had an unexpected extension to Paris. At Harvard, during my last years, there was a rich and isolated student named Caleb Hyde, interested in French literature. On graduating he founded an exchange professorship between Harvard and the Sorbonne, lectures to be in English at Paris, and in French at Cambridge. Barrett Wendell was the first appointed at Paris; and when I was in the East, during 1905, I received an invitation to be his successor. It was most opportune, giving me two years' holiday instead of one; for being in training as a lecturer at that time, and counting on an intelligent audience in Paris, my work there would be easy, and three parts pleasure. So it proved. Never have I talked to so *open* a public—I mean in a course of lectures; singly, I have found an equal openness once or twice in England. Yet, after Wendell, I was a sad disappointment to Hyde and, I suspect, to all the officials concerned. For I avoided seeing anyone, presented none of the letters of introduction that Hyde had sent me by the dozen, and lived in my hotel just as quietly as if I had had no academic duties. I had a reason for this, besides my love of obscurity. The tendency to give a political colour to this lectureship repelled me for two reasons: one, that I was not an American, and was presenting myself, as it were, under false colours; the other, that the political propaganda desired was contrary to my sympathies.

In spite of my avoidance of contacts, I came involuntarily on various little manifestations of the sham and corruption that prevailed in the official world. The most simple avowal of it was made by the Rector of the University of Lille, when on the provincial tour that formed a part of the lecturer's programme, I presented myself and expressed my readiness to give, at his discretion, one or two lectures in English. He raised his hands to heaven, and said quickly: *"Une seule! Il ne faut pas abuser de la fidelité de l'auditoire."* It was fidelity enough in an audience to sit through one lecture without running away. In Paris, in fact, the doors were always open, and slamming, with people coming in late or going away early. I was told of a group of students that peeped in one afternoon. *"Tiens. C'est en Anglais. Filons!"* said the leader, and they all disappeared. This freedom was a little disturbing, yet served to emphasise the sense of security given by the little nucleus of listeners who always came early, smilingly stayed to the end, and evidently understood everything.

Before I set out on my tour of the provincial universities, I had a glimpse of French Government behind the scenes. A young man in a shining red motor burnished like sealing wax turned up at the Foyot, where I lived, and said they wished to speak to me at the Ministry of Public Instruction, and that he would drive me there. I was received by the director of some department, who rang the bell and said that Monsieur So-and-So would explain to me the nature of a request that they desired to make of me. I bowed, said *au revoir, Monsieur,* and followed the secretary into an inner room. This secretary was obsequious, yet in himself, had he been dressed in oriental garments, would have been impressive and almost beautiful. He had a pale complexion, large calm eyes and a long silky black beard falling in two strands. We sat down. He said, with an air of mystery, and perhaps some embarrassment, that in the list of universities that they had selected for me to visit, they had included Lille. Now, there was a special circumstance about Lille to which they wished beforehand to call my attention. At Lille there was also a Catholic Institute. If, going as I did under government direction, I should also address the Catholic Institute, it would cause comment which they desired to avoid. For that reason they had troubled me with this little matter; and they hoped I should understand the position in which they were placed.

I replied that I understood it perfectly, that I had never heard of the Catholic Institute at Lille, had no relations with French Catholic circles, and certainly would not repeat my lecture, at Lille or elsewhere, even if, as was most unlikely, I should be invited to do so. In fact, the Catholic Institute was as oblivious of me as I was of it. But these precautions of the Ministry, and the stealthy hushed tone of them, taught me something of the spirit of the French Government. It was not national, but sectarian. It was afraid that a foreign lecturer should repeat to Catholic students what he had been sent to say to Government students. Apparently —though they paid me nothing, for it was Hyde that paid—they felt that, while I was under their auspices, I was pledged to their policy. If I had known this, or had thought it more than an absurd pretension, I should never have stepped within the Sorbonne.

The last university I visited was that of Lyons, and there pomposity was the order of the day. Everyone was pining for the blessed moment when they should at last be transferred to Paris; but meantime they would pretend that Lyons was the light of the world. I was asked to dinner by the Rector; he said nothing about *sans cérémonie,* and luckily I dressed, for it was an official banquet, forty men, and only one lady, the Rector's wife, in full regalia, next to whom I sat, with the Rector opposite. At the end, with the champagne, my heart sank, for I foresaw that I had to make a speech—my first and last speech in French. Luckily the Rector was very eloquent about the twin republics across the sea, both enlightened, both humane, both progressive, both red-white-and-blue. I had time to think of something to say. I had been hearing and speaking more French than usual, and I managed, not without faults, but decently to express my thanks and to praise the young French universities—younger than Harvard—that I had been visiting. But I also said that, although I was not myself an American, I would convey the friendly sentiments expressed by the Rector to my friends at Harvard, who I knew were inspired by the same feelings. Having relieved my conscience and given them a lesson, I went on more sympathetically and ended without eloquence but with decency. *"Vous avez eu des phrases,"* said one of the guests to me afterwards, *"qui n'étaient pas d'un étranger."* Quite so: the accent may not have been Parisian, but the sentiment was not foreign, because it was human and sincere. We all move together when we pursue the truth.

The last echoes of my official career were posthumous: the professor was dead, the man revived, spoke in the professor's place, and spoke in England. These were all written lectures, and most of them were published in *Character and Opinion in the United States.* Together with *Egotism in German Philosophy* and *Soliloquies in England* they mark my emancipation from official control and professional pretensions. There was no occasion to change my subjects, to abandon even technical philosophy or my interest in academic life and the humanities. But all was now a voluntary study, a satirical survey, a free reconsideration: the point of view had become at once frankly personal and speculatively transcendental. A spirit, the spirit in a stray individual, was settling its accounts with the universe. My official career had happily come to an end.

INDEX

Agatha (Lady Agatha Russell), 42
Aiken, Conrad, 103
Ainger, Canon, *Carmen Etonense*, by, 120
Aingers, the, 120–1
America, 1, 7, 19, 100, 107, 175–6
Americans in Europe, 131–51
Antoñita, Cousin, 76
Apthorp, "Billy," 4
Aristophanes, 24
Aristotle, 157–8
Arnold, Matthew, 19
Atalanta in Calydon, by Swinburne, 45–6
Avila, 76–97, 135, 168–9

Bangs, "Swelly," 99–101, 107
Bank of England, 30–3
Bayley, Edward, 109
Barlow, Bob, 98–101, 107
Barlow, Nelly, 98
Barlow, General, 98
Beal, Boylston, 9, 107–8
Bennett, Miss, 21–2, 27
Berenson, Bernard, 37–9, 58–9
Berenson, Mrs. Bernard, 38–9
Berkeley, Bishop, 178
Berlin, 1, 5, 8–9
Bible in Spain, The, by Borrow, 41
Billings, Emma, 69
Billings, Jennie, 69
Bookbills of Narcissus, The, by Richard Le Gallienne, 45
Borrás, Josefina (author's mother), 112, 158
Borrow, *Bible in Spain*, by, 41
Boston society, 3, 81, 107, 112–30
Bowen, Professor, 153
Brattle Street, No. 60, 12

Bringas, 84–5
Brooks, Phillips, 102
Browning, Robert, 159
Bryn Mawr, 178
Bullard, Frank, 163
Burke, of Trinity, 53–4
Butler, Lawrence, 143–4

Cándido, 78–9
Cape Cod, 101–2, 104
Cape Cod, lines on, by George Santayana, 101–2
Carmen Etonense, by Ainger, 120
Character and Opinion in the United States, by George Santayana, 90, 181
Child, Francis James, 174
Codman, "Cousin" Lucy, 102, 116–7, 121–2
Codman, Julian, 102–4, 108, 117, 121
Codmans, the, 116–7
Colonial Club, 158, 163, 174
Columbia University, 178
Coolidge, "Archie," 162–3
Copeland, Charles Townsend, 173
Cosmic Evolution, by John Fiske, 165
Critique of Practical Reason, by Kant, 7
Cruikshank, George, 19
Cruthers, The Rev. Dr., 164
Cuba, 167
Cuffe, Lady Sybil, 161
Curtis, George William, *Prue and I*, by, 38
Curzon, Lord, 67
Cushing, Howard, 107–8
Cutting, Bayard, 161
Cutting, Iris, 161